The Battle of Dorking

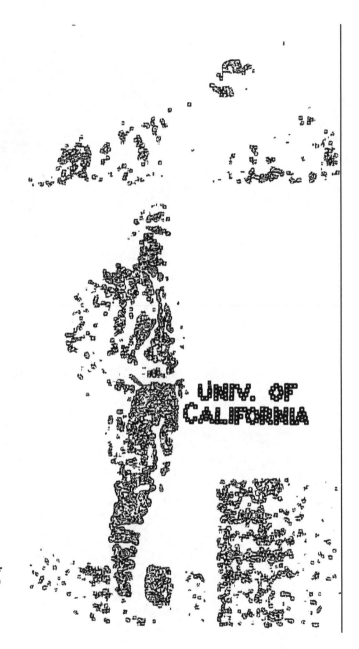

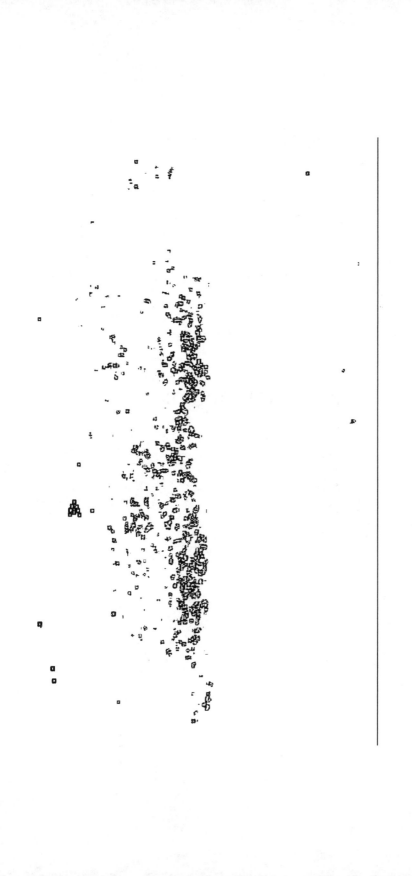

THE BATTLE OF DORKING

THE BATTLE OF
DORKING

WITH AN INTRODUCTION
BY
G. H. POWELL

LONDON
GRANT RICHARDS LTD.
MDCCCCXIV

PREFACE

THE warnings and prophecies addressed to one
generation must prove very ineffective if they are
equally applicable to the next. But in the eloquent
appeal published forty-three years ago, by General
Chesney, with its vivid description and harrowing
pathos, few readers will not recognize parallel
features to those of our own situation in Septem-
ber, 1914.

True the handicaps of the invasion of August,
1871, are heavily piled upon the losing combatant.
Not only the eternal Anglo-Irish trouble (so easily
mistaken by the foreigner for such a difference as
might be found separating two other countries)
but complications with America, as well as the
common form seduction of the British fleet to the
Dardanelles, a general unreadiness of all administrative departments, and a deep distrust of the
" volunteer " movement, involve the whole drama
in an atmosphere of profound pessimism.

But there are scores of other details, counsels,
and reflections (of which we will not spoil the
reader's enjoyment by anticipation) which, as the
common saying is of history when it repeats itself,
" might have been written yesterday." The

desperate condition of things is all the more remarkable as Englishmen had just witnessed the crushing defeat of their great ally—supposed to be the first military power of Europe—by the enemy they are supposed to despise. The story is otherwise simple enough. The secret annexation of Holland and Denmark is disclosed. People said we might have kept out of the trouble. But an impulsive nation egged on the Government who, confident that our old luck would pull us through, at once declare war. The fleet, trying to close with the enemy, is destroyed in " a few minutes " by the " deadly engines " left behind by the evasive enemy; our amateurish armies are defeated on our own soil, and *voilà tout.*

Remarkable must have been the national insouciance, or despondent the eye which viewed it, to explain the impassioned actuality of such a *reveillematin.*

For one thing it may be remarked that *The Battle of Dorking,** though in a sense the "history" of the pamphlet is already " ancient," is really the first of its kind. The topic, then of such inspiring freshness, has since become well worn.

Mutatis mutandis, doubtless, much of General Chesney's advice and warning might have been repeated on the occasion of the Boer War. If that were not a practical " alarum to the patriotic

---

* Contributed by Genl Sir Geo T. Chesney (1830-1895) to *Blackwood's Magazine* (May, 1871) It created a great sensation and appeared in pamphlet form the same year

Briton," we ask ourselves what could be so called. Perhaps it combined the maximum of alarm with the minimum of national risk, but its beneficent influence can scarcely be questioned.

At the date of the republication of this pamphlet we face a peril immeasurably greater than that, if not equal to the Napoleonic terror of 1803 ; and we face it, as concerns the mass of our population, with a calmness which—to critical eyes and in view of the appeal made by the Government to the country—is at least susceptible of an unsatisfactory explanation.

If surprise, misunderstanding, may in a measure account for that, it would be idle to pretend that the national mood and temper (and the moods and tempers of nations will vary) were altogether —if they could ever be—such as encouraged the most sanguine hopes of our success when exposed to an ordeal of suddenness, extent, and severity unknown in the world's history.

In estimating the risks of our situation, thoughtful criticism may be said to run naturally into two channels.

Firstly, in the political world—for reasons which cannot here be considered—the past decade has seen a predominance of idealist activity and ratiocination scarcely known before.

Hence the State has exhibited, to some extent, a *Utopiste* attitude likely to mislead foreign nations—it may be said with mild brevity—alike as to our real views of their conduct, and as to our national belief in the right or duty of self-assertion.

If, in 1871, we were represented as the helpless dupes of foreign diplomacy, in 1914 we rather appear to have deceived the enemy to our own hurt. A humane aversion to War—though, for that matter, it is only by a philanthropic "illusion" that the extreme stage of self-assertion can be morally differentiated from those that precede it, may tempt politicians by a too sedulous avoidance of the unpleasing phrase to invite the dreadful reality. But, again, in the private life of the nation, other traits (some noted in the pamphlet of '71) have given cause for critical reflection. Besides Luxury—remarkable enough in its novel and fantastic forms, though a commonplace complaint of tractarians in all ages—a generally increased relaxation of all old-established ties of religion, convention or tradition, a tendency noticeable in general conduct, art and letters alike, a sort of orgy of intellectual and literary Erastianism, a *blasé* craving for sensational novelty (encouraged perhaps if not sated by the startling novelties of the age) have given scope for anxiety as to the conservation in the English nature of that solid *morale*, that "gesundes und sicheres Gefühl" defined by an eminent thinker as the source of all worthy activity.

These words can but very crudely sketch a complex sense of uneasiness and dissatisfaction familiar to most of us.

Mr. Kipling has sung long since of athletic

excesses and indolence. More recent critics have
dwelt on the extravagant time and expense
devoted to golf. General Chesney would have
branded the sensationalist effeminacy of our
football-gloating crowds of thousands who might
be recruits. Reviewers laugh wearily over the
horrors or absurdities of the latest poetic mon-
strosity or "futurist" nightmare. But in one
phase or another the consciousness is present to
all, and not unnoticed by our enemies.

And it adds a sting to our inevitable anxiety if
we cannot yet feel sure how far we can "recollect"
our true best selves in the very moment of action,
how far there has been given to us that saving
grace of a storm-tost nation, "*l'art de porter en soi
le remède de ses propres défauts.*"

Every race, doubtless, has its own special
weaknesses and delusions, the "idols" of its
patriotic "cave," and it is a commonplace of
history that the moral, physical, or intellectual
"decadence" of one age is revived and actualized
by the material cataclysm of another.

And the readiness, spiritual and material, of the
nation *in utrumque paratus* is the index of its
harmony with its environment.

On the other hand there are wars to be fully
prepared for which would almost mean to be a
partner in their criminality. There is an attitude
of defence which, if successful, would lose all
dignity were it allied with a permanent distrust in
the morality and humanity of other nations.

If only an inhuman pride could be free from
uneasiness at such a moment; at least warm
encouragement comes to us *ab extra.* Whatever
our weaknesses now, our sins or blunders in the
past, no historian will question the motive, nay,
the severe moral effort with which the English
nation enters upon this war of the ages.

It is scarcely conceivable that any people could
be called upon to make a greater or more sudden
exhibition of—their peculiar qualities.

What will be the verdict upon our own? That
we are wilfully misunderstood, misrepresented,
must matter little to us, if we have the moral
support of a public opinion which will, if we
triumph, be more powerful for good than ever
before.

Nor need we fear its ultimate perversion by
interested slander. The hostile demonstrations of
the German intellect during the early stages of this
war have scarcely been on a par with those of its
material force.

One of the latest of sophistical Imperialist
ebullitions complains with somewhat forced pathos
of our waging war with our former allies of
Waterloo!

But we did not fight the French then because
they were French, nor ally ourselves with
Prussians because they spoke a guttural tongue.
We fought then, as now, against the erection of
an impossible and unbearable European tyranny,
the local origin and nationality of which would

have been quite immaterial to the main question. Can we believe for a moment that the great German intellect has ever been under the slightest misapprehension of so very simple a matter? War, honest war, may be Hell, as General Sherman described it. It is, at least, a form of Purgatory in which personality, nationality, are forces that count but little, while principle and motive (as was tragically exhibited in the great American struggle) are everything. Did not Christianity itself preach this kind of sanctified discord in which a novel sense of right, or the perception of higher ideal, should divide even the nearest and dearest, and set them at war not, as in old days, by reason of any " family compact," or mere racial tie, but for the sake of " Right," and—so far as ordinary friendly or neighbourly relations were concerned—in utter " scorn of consequence."

There, indeed, is the poignant tragedy of the case. To be at war with the countrymen of Schumann and Beethoven, of Goethe and Ranke, is not that an affliction to the very soul of England, an outrage to feelings and instincts tangled up with the very core of our civilization?

Terrible, indeed, is it that there should be amities which, at such crises, we must

> " tear from our bosom
> Though our heart be at the root."

No man or nation expects perfection in his friends. Honestly we have loved and respected the German. We have not wormed ourselves into his confidence, nursing through long years secret stores of explosive jealousy. His art, his learning, have had their full meed of admiration from his kindred here.

But, we recognize—dull, indeed, would they be who needed a more striking reminder that beneath the defective " manner " of the Teuton lurks an element of crude barbarity with which we cannot pretend to fraternize.

The violence of the Goths and Huns had its place in history ; but that would be a strange international morality which would give the rein now to mediæval instincts of egoistic tyranny and perfectly organized brute force, as against the gentler instincts, the higher social civilization largely associated with the Latin and Celtic races.

In these matters the Balance of Power is no less vital to international life and the evolution of true cosmopolitan ideals than in mere Politics. And if we stand up in battle for the smaller races it is not merely because they are small and need defence, but because an element of the right, a share in the civilization which we mean to prevail, is with them and a part of their heritage.

The technical bond may be, as the scoffing enemy remarks (in words which will surely, as curses, return some day to roost), a mere " scrap of paper " signed with England's name.

But the civilized world will recognize that it is only by the increased sanctity of such ties that

Europe advances towards intelligent cosmopoli-
tanism, and leaves behind the vandal wild beast
den after which woe to those who still hanker!

* * * *

There were critics, even English critics, who
have taken so superficial a view of history and
humanity, as to ask why we should support,
France, with our blood and treasure, when in
morale and intellect it is perhaps the candid truth
that we are more on the side of her enemy.

It is scarcely necessary to urge in reply that
France, if not the one great continental nation, is
the one great people of parallel and contemporary
development to our own, our comrade, our rival,
our nearest social (if not racial) kin, and that, spite
of all her decadence and even degradation, upon
the arena of Europe she stands for Humanity and
Civilization against Absolutism and Brute Force.
And as we raised the world against her, when
dominated by the tyrannous egoism of Bona-
parte, the monstrous fungoid growth that over-
laid her great Revolution and obscured her
services to freedom, so now we stand as foes, not,
we would fain believe, of the German people, but
of the militarist clique, the Napoleonic nightmare
that overpowers her moral instincts and clouds
her honesty and intelligence. But here, again, let
us not deceive ourselves as to the extent—perhaps
to be all too fatally revealed—of "the force behind
the Kaiser." Germany of to-day stands for a
compact mass of highly energized (though not yet

politically conscious) material and intellectual
vigour. That a group of principalities, obsessed
by militarist and petty-aristocratic traditions,
should within half a century of their amalgama-
tion form a politically great and united people,
could scarcely be expected.

But if not fully organized on the representative
lines to which we attach so much importance,
Germany presents a united front of intelligence,
commercial industry and ambition with which her
rapidly increasing population pushes on, eager for
new worlds to conquer.

That she demands an " Elizabethan age " of her
own is the tragic platitude of our time.

That she is aggrieved that we have had one,
while we can only imperfectly (in her estimation)
utilize its modern fruits, is her true theoretical
casus belli against us.

The immorality of the position consists in her
belief that the Sun of Civilization must stand still,
the currents of Law and Order run backwards to
satisfy her *entêtée* and unscrupulous jealousy.
Englishmen have been so innocent as to believe
she would be satisfied by a share, nay an extensive
monopoly of the trade we once thought our own.
They have urged that the German has all the
advantages enjoyed by a native throughout the
British Empire, that in spite of a constant agita-
tion by a large and powerful party, no English
Government has ever used its power to impose
any artificial restraints upon German trade ; that

the fullest hospitality of these Islands has been
extended to our Teuton brethren ; while they were
invited to successfully compete on their merits
with one English industry after another.

That they would not rest content with these
advantages, this political and commercial equality,
that they would want to organize secret treachery,
to spy out our weaknesses and hide bombs in their
bedrooms, that—to the simple Briton of a few
weeks ago—would have seemed impossible.

He now knows what primitive passions may
lurk behind a plausible commercialism secretly
disappointed in its immoderate greed.

It is in the alliance of despotic militarism with
bureaucratic intellectual sophistry that has lain
a new peril for the world; and one yet to be fully
realized by the German people, when many of the
hasty and speculative structures of her self-
conscious and academic Protectionism are dis-
covered to be as unsound as the quasi-religious
aphorisms of the Kaiser.

In spite of these confident assurances it may be
the fate of that arrogant leader to find himself at
war with " things," stony facts, economic laws
that crush the transgressor, as well as with an
indignant world.

Meanwhile—our armies have fought bravely
and held their own in the greatest battle, the
most ferocious conflict the world ever dreamed of.

Our unconquered fleet, after the tradition of
four centuries, is still " looking for the enemy."

All around us, as we write, is evidence that the nation is bracing herself for a new and stupendous effort of courage, perhaps of imaginative strategy and even *Weltpolitik* which will in startling fashion bring the forces of half the world to meet and crush a world-menacing peril, and place our England, the mistress of the seas, on a pinnacle where she will be justified of all her patriotic children, counsellors, critics and heroes alike.

G. H. POWELL.

THE BATTLE OF DORKING

You ask me to tell you, my grandchildren, something about my own share in the great events that happened fifty years ago. 'Tis sad work turning back to that bitter page in our history, but you may perhaps take profit in your new homes from the lesson it teaches. For us in England it came too late. And yet we had plenty of warnings, if we had only made use of them. The danger did not come on us unawares: It burst on us suddenly, 'tis true; but its coming was foreshadowed plainly enough to open our eyes, if we had not been wilfully blind. We English have only ourselves to blame for the humiliation which has been brought on the land. Venerable old age! Dishonourable old age, I say, when it follows a manhood dishonoured as ours has been. I declare, even now, though fifty years have passed, I can hardly look a young man in the face when I think I am one of those in whose youth happened this degradation of Old England—one of those who betrayed the trust handed down to us unstained by our fore-fathers.

What a proud and happy country was this

B

fifty years ago! Free-trade had been working for
more than a quarter of a century, and there
seemed to be no end to the riches it was bringing
us. London was growing bigger and bigger ; you
could not build houses fast enough for the rich
people who wanted to live in them, the merchants
who made the money and came from all parts of
the world to settle there, and the lawyers and
doctors and engineers and others, and trades-
people who got their share out of the profits. The
streets reached down to Croydon and Wimbledon,
which my father could remember quite country
places ; and people used to say that Kingston and
Reigate would soon be joined to London. We
thought we could go on building and multiplying
for ever. 'Tis true that even then there was no
lack of poverty ; the people who had no money
went on increasing as fast as the rich, and pauperism was already beginning to be a difficulty ; but
if the rates were high, there was plenty of money
to pay them with ; and as for what were called the
middle classes, there really seemed no limit to their
increase and prosperity. People in those days
thought it quite a matter of course to bring a
dozen children into the world—or, as it used to be
said, Providence sent them that number of babies;
and if they couldn't always marry off all the daugh-
ters, they used to manage to provide for the sons,
for there were new openings to be found in all the
professions, or in the Government offices, which
went on steadily getting larger. Besides, in those

days young men could be sent out to India, or into
the army or navy; and even then emigration was
not uncommon, although not the regular custom
it is now. Schoolmasters, like all other profes-
sional classes, drove a capital trade. They did
not teach very much, to be sure, but new schools
with their four or five hundred boys were springing
up all over the country.

Fools that we were! We thought that all this
wealth and prosperity were sent us by Providence,
and could not stop coming. In our blindness we
did not see that we were merely a big workshop,
making up the things which came from all parts
of the world; and that if other nations stopped
sending us raw goods to work up, we could not
produce them ourselves. True, we had in those
days an advantage in our cheap coal and iron; and
had we taken care not to waste the fuel, it might
have lasted us longer. But even then there were
signs that coal and iron would soon become
cheaper in foreign parts; while as to food and
other things, England was not better off than it is
now. We were so rich simply because other nations from all parts of the world were in the habit
of sending their goods to us to be sold or manu-
factured; and we thought that this would last for
ever. And so, perhaps, it might have lasted, if we
had only taken proper means to keep it; but, in
our folly, we were too careless even to insure our
prosperity, and after the course of trade was
turned away it would not come back again.

And yet, if ever a nation had a plain warning,
we had. If we were the greatest trading country,
our neighbours were the leading military power in
Europe. They were driving a good trade, too, for
this was before their foolish communism (about
which you will hear when you are older) had
ruined the rich without benefiting the poor, and
they were in many respects the first nation in
Europe; but it was on their army that they
prided themselves most. And with reason. They
had beaten the Russians and the Austrians, and
the Prussians too, in bygone years, and they
thought they were invincible. Well do I remember the great review held at Paris by the Emperor
Napoleon during the great Exhibition, and how
proud he looked showing off his splendid Guards
to the assembled kings and princes. Yet, three
years afterwards, the force so long deemed the
first in Europe was ignominiously beaten, and the
whole army taken prisoners. Such a defeat had
never happened before in the world's history;
and with this proof before us of the folly of dis-
believing in the possibility of disaster merely because it had never fallen upon us, it might have
been supposed that we should have the sense to
take the lesson to heart. And the country was
certainly roused for a time, and a cry was raised
that the army ought to be reorganized, and our
defences strengthened against the enormous power
for sudden attacks which it was seen other nations were able to put forth. And a scheme of

army reform was brought forward by the Government. It was a half-and-half affair at best; and
unfortunately, instead of being taken up in Parliament as a national scheme, it was made a party
matter of, and so fell through. There was a
Radical section of the House, too, whose votes
had to be secured by conciliation, and which
blindly demanded a reduction of armaments as
the price of allegiance. This party always decried
military establishments as part of a fixed policy
for reducing the influence of the Crown and the
aristocracy. They could not understand that the
times had altogether changed, that the Crown had
really no power, and that the Government merely
existed at the pleasure of the House of Commons,
and that even Parliament-rule was beginning to
give way to mob-law. At any rate, the Ministry,
baffled on all sides, gave up by degrees all the
strong points of a scheme which they were not
heartily in earnest about. It was not that there
was any lack of money; if only it had been spent
in the right way. The army cost enough, and
more than enough, to give us a proper defence,
and there were armed men of sorts in plenty and
to spare, if only they had been decently organized.
It was in organization and forethought that we
fell short, because our rulers did not heartily believe in the need for preparation. The fleet and
the Channel, they said, were sufficient protection.
So army reform was put off to some more con-
venient season, and the militia and volunteers

were left untrained as before, because to call them
out for drill would "interfere with the industry
of the country." We could have given up some of
the industry of those days, forsooth, and yet be
busier than we are now. But why tell you a tale
you have so often heard already? The nation,
although uneasy, was misled by the false security
its leaders professed to feel; and the warning
given by the disasters that overtook France was
allowed to pass by unheeded. We would not even
be at the trouble of putting our arsenals in a safe
place, or of guarding the capital against a surprise,
although the cost of doing so would not have been
so much as missed from the national wealth. The
French trusted in their army and its great repu-
tation, we in our fleet; and in each case the result
of this blind confidence was disaster, such as our
forefathers in their hardest struggles could not
have even imagined.

I need hardly tell you how the crash came about.
First, the rising in India drew away a part of our
small army; then came the difficulty with
America, which had been threatening for years,
and we sent off ten thousand men to defend
Canada—a handful which did not go far to
strengthen the real defences of that country, but
formed an irresistible temptation to the Ameri-
cans to try and take them prisoners, especially as
the contingent included three battalions of the
Guards. Thus the regular army at home was even
smaller than usual, and nearly half of it was in

Ireland to check the talked-of Fenian invasion fitting out in the West. Worse still—though I do not know it would really have mattered as things turned out—the fleet was scattered abroad : some ships to guard the West Indies, others to check privateering in the China seas, and a large part to try and protect our colonies on the Northern Pacific shore of America; where; with incredible folly, we continued to retain possessions which we could not possibly defend. America was not the great power forty years ago that it is now ; but for us to try and hold territory on her shores which could only be reached by sailing round the Horn, was as absurd as if she had attempted to take the Isle of Man before the independence of Ireland. We see this plainly enough now, but we were all blind then.

It was while we were in this state, with our ships all over the world, and our little bit of an army cut up into detachments, that the Secret Treaty was published, and Holland and Denmark were annexed. People say now that we might have escaped the troubles which came on us if we had at any rate kept quiet till our other difficulties were settled ; but the English were always an impulsive lot : the whole country was boiling over with indignation, and the Government, egged on by the Press, and going with the stream, declared war. We had always got out of scrapes before, and we believed our old luck and pluck would somehow pull us through.

Then, of course, there was bustle and hurry all over the land. Not that the calling up of the army reserves caused much stir, for I think there were only about 5,000 altogether, and a good many of these were not to be found when the time came; but recruiting was going on all over the country, with a tremendous high bounty, 50,000 more men having been voted for the army. Then there was a a Ballot Bill passed for adding 55,500 men to the militia; why a round number was not fixed on I don't know, but the Prime Minister said that this was the exact quota wanted to put the defences of the country on a sound footing. Then the ship-building that began! Ironclads, despatch-boats, gunboats, monitors,—every building-yard in the country got its job, and they were offering ten shillings a day wages for anybody who could drive a rivet. This didn't improve the recruiting, you may suppose. I remember, too, there was a squabble in the House of Commons about whether artisans should be drawn for the ballot, as they were so much wanted, and I think they got an exemption. This sent numbers to the yards; and if we had had a couple of years to prepare instead of a couple of weeks, I daresay we should have done very well.

It was on a Monday that the declaration of war was announced, and in a few hours we got our first inkling of the sort of preparation the enemy had made for the event which they had really brought about, although the actual declaration was made by us. A pious appeal to the God of battles, whom it was said we had aroused, was telegraphed back; and from that moment all communication with the north of Europe was cut off. Our embassies and legations were packed off at an hour's notice, and it was as if we had suddenly come back to the middle ages. The dumb astonishment visible all over London the next morning, when the papers came out void of news, merely hinting at what had happened, was one of the most startling things in this war of surprises. But everything had been arranged beforehand; nor ought we to have been surprised, for we had seen the same Power, only a few months before, move down half a million of men on a few days' notice, to conquer the greatest military nation in Europe, with no more fuss than our War Office used to make over the transport of a brigade from Aldershot to Brighton,—and this, too, without the allies it had now. What happened now was not a bit more wonderful in reality; but people of this country could not bring themselves to believe that what had never occurred before to England could ever possibly happen. Like our neighbours, we became wise when it was too late.

Of course the papers were not long in getting news—even the mighty organization set at work could not shut out a special correspondent; and in a very few days, although the telegraphs and railways were intercepted right across Europe, the main facts oozed out. An embargo had been laid on all the shipping in every port from the Baltic to Ostend; the fleets of the two great Powers had moved out, and it was supposed were assembled in the great northern harbour, and troops were hurrying on board all the steamers detained in these places, most of which were British vessels. It was clear that invasion was intended. Even then we might have been saved, if the fleet had been ready. The forts which guarded the flotilla were perhaps too strong for shipping to attempt; but an ironclad or two, handled as British sailors knew how to use them, might have destroyed or damaged a part of the transports, and delayed the expedition, giving us what we wanted, time. But then the best part of the fleet had been decoyed down to the Dardanelles, and what remained of the Channel squadron was looking after Fenian fili-busters off the west of Ireland; so it was ten days before the fleet was got together, and by that time it was plain the enemy's preparations were too far advanced to be stopped by a *coup-de-main*. Information, which came chiefly through Italy, came slowly, and was more or less vague and un-certain; but this much was known, that at least a couple of hundred thousand men were em-barked or ready to be put on board ships; and that the flotilla was guarded by more ironclads than we could then muster. I suppose it was the un-certainty as to the point the enemy would aim at for landing, and the fear lest he should give us the the go-by, that kept the fleet for several days in

the Downs; but it was not until the Tuesday
fortnight after the declaration of war that it
weighed anchor and steamed away for the North
Sea. Of course you have read about the Queen's
visit to the fleet the day before, and how she
sailed round the ships in her yacht, and went on
board the flag-ship to take leave of the admiral;
how, overcome with emotion, she told him that
the safety of the country was committed to his
keeping. You remember, too, the gallant old
officer's reply, and how all the ships' yards were
manned, and how lustily the tars cheered as her
Majesty was rowed off. The account was of course
telegraphed to London, and the high spirits of the
fleet infected the whole town. I was outside the
Charing Cross station when the Queen's special
train from Dover arrived, and from the cheering
and shouting which greeted her Majesty as she
drove away, you might have supposed we had
already won a great victory. The leading journal,
which had gone in strongly for the army reduction
carried out during the session, and had been
nervous and desponding in tone during the past
fortnight, suggesting all sorts of compromises as a
way of getting out of the war, came out in a very
jubilant form next morning. "Panic-stricken
inquirers," it said, "ask now, where are the means
of meeting the invasion? We reply that the invasion will never take place. A British fleet
manned by British sailors, whose courage and
enthusiasm are reflected in the people of this

country, is already on the way to meet the presumptuous foe. The issue of a contest between British ships and those of any other country, under anything like equal odds, can never be doubtful. England awaits with calm confidence the issue of the impending action."

Such were the words of the leading article, and so we all felt. It was on Tuesday, the 10th of August, that the fleet sailed from the Downs. It took with it a submarine cable to lay down as it advanced, so that continuous communication was kept up, and the papers were publishing special editions every few minutes with the latest news. This was the first time such a thing had been done and the feat was accepted as a good omen. Whether it is true that the Admiralty made use of the cable to keep on sending contradictory orders, which took the command out of the admiral's hands, I can't say; but all that the admiral sent in return was a few messages of the briefest kind, which neither the Admiralty nor any one else could have made any use of. Such a ship had gone off reconnoitring; such another had rejoined —fleet was in latitude so and so. This went on till the Thursday morning. I had just come up to town by train as usual, and was walking to my office, when the newsboys began to cry, "New edition—enemy's fleet in sight!" You may imagine the scene in London! Business still went on at the banks, for bills matured although the independence of the country was being fought out

under our own eyes, so to say, and the speculators
were active enough. But even with the people
who were making and losing their fortunes, the
interest in the fleet overcame everything else;
men who went to pay in or draw out their money
stopped to show the last bulletin to the cashier.
As for the street, you could hardly get along for
the crowd stopping to buy and read the papers;
while at every house or office the members sat
restlessly in the common room, as if to keep together for company, sending out some one of their
number every few minutes to get the latest edition. At least this is what happened at our office;
but to sit still was as impossible as to do anything,
and most of us went out and wandered about
among the crowd, under a sort of feeling that the
news was got quicker at in this way. Bad as were
the times coming, I think the sickening suspense
of that day, and the shock which followed, was
almost the worst that we underwent. It was about
ten o'clock that the first telegram came; an hour
later the wire announced that the admiral had
signalled to form line of battle, and shortly afterwards that the order was given to bear down on
the enemy and engage. At twelve came the
announcement, "Fleet opened fire about three
miles to leeward of us "—that is, the ship with the
cable. So far all had been expectancy, then came
the first token of calamity. " An ironclad has
been blown up "—" the enemy's torpedoes are
doing great damage "—" the flagship is laid

aboard the enemy."—"the flag-ship appears to
be sinking."—"the vice-admiral has signalled to"
—there the cable became silent, and, as you know,
we heard no more till, two days afterwards, the
solitary ironclad which escaped the disaster
steamed into Portsmouth.

Then the whole story came out—how our sailors
gallant as ever, had tried to close with the enemy ;
how the latter evaded the conflict at close quarters, and, sheering off, left behind them the fatal
engines which sent our ships, one after the other,
to the bottom ; how all this happened almost in a
few minutes. The Government, it appears, had
received warnings of this invention ; but to the
nation this stunning blow was utterly unexpected.
That Thursday I had to go home early for regi-
mental drill, but it was impossible to remain doing
nothing, so when that was over I went up to town
again, and after waiting in expectation of news
which never came, and missing the midnight
train, I walked home. It was a hot sultry night,
and I did not arrive till near sunrise. The whole
town was quite still—the lull before the storm;
and as I let myself in with my latch-key, and went
softly upstairs to my room to avoid waking the
sleeping household, I could not but contrast the
peacefulness of the morning—no sound breaking
the silence but the singing of the birds in the garden—with the passionate remorse and indignation
that would break out with the day. Perhaps the
inmates of the rooms were as wakeful as myself ;

but the house in its stillness was just as it used to be
when I came home alone from balls or parties in
the happy days gone by. Tired though I was, I
could not sleep, so I went down to the river and
had a swim; and on returning found the household was assembling for early breakfast. A sor-
rowful household it was, although the burden
pressing on each was partly an unseen one. My
father, doubting whether his firm could last
through the day; my mother, her distress about
my brother, now with his regiment on the coast,
already exceeding that which she felt for the
public misfortune, had come down, although
hardly fit to leave her room. My sister Clara was
worst of all, for she could not but try to disguise
her special interest in the fleet; and though we
had all guessed that her heart was given to the
young lieutenant in the flag-ship—the first vessel
to go down—a love unclaimed could not be told,
nor could we express the sympathy we felt for the
poor girl. That breakfast, the last meal we ever
had together, was soon ended, and my father and
I went up to town by an early train, and got there
just as the fatal announcement of the loss of the
fleet was telegraphed from Portsmouth.

The panic and excitement of that day—how the
funds went down to 35; the run upon the bank
and its stoppage; the fall of half the houses in the
city; how the Government issued a notification
suspending specie payment and the tendering of
bills—this last precaution too late for most firms,

Graham & Co. among the number, which stopped
payment as soon as my father got to the office ;
the call to arms and the unanimous response of
the country—all this is history which I need not
repeat. You wish to hear about my own share in
the business of the time. Well, volunteering had
increased immensely from the day war was pro-
claimed, and our regiment went up in a day or two
from its usual strength of 600 to nearly 1,000. But
the stock of rifles was deficient. We were promised a further supply in a few days, which however, we never received ; and while waiting for
them the regiment had to be divided into two
parts, the recruits drilling with the rifles in the
morning, and we old hands in the evening. The
failures and stoppage of work on this black Friday
threw an immense number of young men out of
employment, and we recruited up to 1,400 strong
by the next day ; but what was the use of all these
men without arms ? On the Saturday it was announced that a lot of smooth-bore muskets in store
at the Tower would be served out to regiments
applying for them, and a regular scramble took
place among the volunteers for them, and our
people got hold of a couple of hundred. But you
might almost as well have tried to learn rifle-drill
with a broom-stick as with old brown bess ;
besides, there was no smooth-bore ammunition
in the country. A national subscription was
opened for the manufacture of rifles at Birmingham, which ran up to a couple of millions in two

days, but, like everything else, this came too late.
To return to the volunteers : camps had been
formed a fortnight before at Dover, Brighton,
Harwich, and other places, of regulars and militia,
and the headquarters of most of the volunteer
regiments were attached to one or other of them,
and the volunteers themselves used to go down for
drill from day to day, as they could spare time,
and on Friday an order went out that they should
be permanently embodied ; but the metropolitan
volunteers were still kept about London as a sort
of reserve, till it could be seen at what point the
invasion would take place. We were all told off to
brigades and divisions. Our brigade consisted of
the 4th Royal Surrey Militia, the 1st Surrey
Administrative Battalion, as it was called, at
Clapham, the 7th Surrey Volunteers at South-
wark, and ourselves ; but only our battalion and
the militia were quartered in the same place, and
the whole brigade had merely two or three after-
noons together at brigade exercise in Bushey Park
before the march took place. Our brigadier belonged to a line regiment in Ireland, and did not
join till the very morning the order came. Meanwhile, during the preliminary fortnight, the militia
colonel commanded. But though we volunteers
were busy with our drill and preparations, those of
us who, like myself, belonged to Government offices,
had more than enough of office work to do, as you
may suppose. The volunteer clerks were allowed
to leave office at four o'clock, but the rest were

c

kept hard at the desk far into the night. Orders
to the lord-lieutenants, to the magistrates; noti-
fications, all the arrangements for cleaning out the
workhouses for hospitals—these and a hundred
other things had to be managed in our office, and
there was as much bustle indoors as out. Fortu-
nate we were to be so busy—the people to be
pitied were those who had nothing to do. And on
Sunday (that was the 15th August) work went on
just as usual. We had an early parade and drill,
and I went up to town by the nine o'clock train in
my uniform, taking my rifle with me in case of
accidents, and luckily too, as it turned out, a
mackintosh overcoat. When I got to Waterloo
there were all sorts of rumours afloat. A fleet had
been seen off the Downs, and some of the despatch-
boats which were hovering about the coasts
brought news that there was a large flotilla off
Harwich, but nothing could be seen from the
shore, as the weather was hazy. The enemy's
light ships had taken and sunk all the fishing
boats they could catch, to prevent the news of
their whereabouts reaching us ; but a few escaped
during the night and reported that the Inconstant
frigate coming home from North America without
any knowledge of what had taken place, had
sailed right into the enemy's fleet and been captured. In town the troops were all getting ready
for a move ; the Guards in the Wellington Bar-
racks were under arms, and their baggage-waggons packed and drawn up in the Bird-cage Walk.

The usual guard at the Horse Guards had been
withdrawn, and orderlies and staff-officers were
going to and fro. All this I saw on the way to my
office, where I worked away till twelve o'clock,
and then feeling hungry after my early breakfast,
I went across Parliament Street to my club to get
some luncheon. There were about half-a-dozen
men in the coffee-room, none of whom I knew;
but in a minute or two Danvers of the Treasury
entered in a tremendous hurry. From him I got
the first bit of authentic news I had had that day.
The enemy had landed in force near Harwich, and
the metropolitan regiments were ordered down
there to reinforce the troops already collected in
that neighbourhood ; his regiment was to parade
at one o'clock, and he had come to get something
to eat before starting. We bolted a hurried lunch,
and were just leaving the club when a messenger
from the Treasury came running into the hall.

"Oh, Mr. Danvers," said he, "I've come to
look for you, sir ; the secretary says that all the
gentlemen are wanted at the office, and that you
must please not one of you go with the regiments."

"The devil!" cried Danvers.

"Do you know if that order extends to all the
public offices?" I asked.

"I don't know," said the man, "but I believe
it do. I know there's messengers gone round to all
the clubs and luncheon-bars to look for the gentlemen ; the secretary says it's quite impossible any
one can be spared just now, there's so much work

to do; there's orders just come to send off our
records to Birmingham to-night."

I did not wait to condole with Danvers, but,
just glancing up Whitehall to see if any of our
messengers were in pursuit, I ran off as hard as I
could for Westminster Bridge, and so to the
Waterloo station.

The place had quite changed its aspect since the
morning. The regular service of trains had ceased,
and the station and approaches were full of troops,
among them the Guards and artillery. Everything was very orderly: the men had piled arms,
and were standing about in groups. There was no
sign of high spirits or enthusiasm. Matters had
become too serious. Every man's face reflected
the general feeling that we had neglected the
warnings given us, and that now the danger so
long derided as impossible and absurd had really
come and found us unprepared. But the soldiers,
if grave, looked determined, like men who meant
to do their duty whatever might happen. A train
full of guardsmen was just starting for Guildford.
I was told it would stop at Surbiton, and, with
several other volunteers, hurrying like myself to
join our regiment, got a place in it. We did not
arrive a moment too soon, for the regiment was
marching from Kingston down to the station. The
destination of our brigade was the east coast.
Empty carriages were drawn up in the siding, and
our regiment was to go first. A large crowd was
assembled to see it off, including the recruits who

had joined during the last fortnight,- and who formed by far the largest part of our strength. They were to stay behind, and were certainly very much in the way already; for as all the officers and sergeants belonged to the active part, there was no one to keep discipline among them, and they came crowding around us, breaking the ranks and making it difficult to get into the train. Here I saw our new brigadier for the first time. He was a soldier-like man, and no doubt knew his duty, but he appeared new to volunteers, and did not seem to know how to deal with gentlemen privates. I wanted very much to run home and get my greatcoat and knapsack, which I had bought a few days ago, but feared to be left behind; a good-natured recruit volunteered to fetch them for me; but he had not returned before we started, and I began the campaign with a kit consisting of a mackintosh and a small pouch of tobacco.

It was a tremendous squeeze in the train; for, besides the ten men sitting down, there were three or four standing up in every compartment, and the afternoon was close and sultry, and there were so many stoppages on the way that we took nearly an hour and a half crawling up to Waterloo. It was between five and six in the afternoon when we arrived there, and it was nearly seven before we marched up to the Shoreditch station. The whole place was filled up with stores and ammunition, to be sent off to the east, so we piled arms in the street and scattered about to get food and

drink, of which most of us stood in need, especially
the latter, for some were already feeling the worse
for the heat and crush. I was just stepping into a
public-house with Travers, when who should drive
up but his pretty wife? Most of our friends had
paid their adieus at the Surbiton station, but she
had driven up by the road in his brougham, bringing their little boy to have a last look at papa. She
had also brought his knapsack and greatcoat, and,
what was still more acceptable, a basket containing fowls, tongue, bread-and-butter, and biscuits,
and a couple of bottles of claret,—which priceless
luxuries they insisted on, my sharing.

. Meanwhile the hours went on. The 4th Surrey
Militia, which had marched all the way from
Kingston, had come up, as well as the other volunteer corps ;- the station had been partly cleared of
the stores that encumbered it ; some artillery,
two militia regiments, and a battalion of the line,
had been despatched, and our turn to start had
come, and long lines of carriages were drawn up
ready for us ; but still we remained in the street.
You may fancy the scene. There seemed to be as
many people as ever in London, and we could
hardly move for the crowds of spectators—fellows
hawking fruits and volunteers' comforts, newsboys and so forth, to say nothing of the cabs and
omnibuses ; while orderlies and staff-officers were
constantly riding up with messages. A good many
of the militiamen, and some of our people too,
had taken more than enough to drink ; perhaps a

hot sun had told on empty stomachs; anyhow,
they became very noisy. The din, dirt, and heat
were indescribable. So the evening wore on, and
all the information our officers could get from the
brigadier, who appeared to be acting under another
general, was, that orders had come to stand fast
for the present. Gradually the street became
quieter and cooler. The brigadier, who, by way of
setting an example, had remained for some hours
without leaving his saddle, had got a chair out of a
shop, and sat nodding in it; most of the men were
lying down or sitting on the pavement—some
sleeping, some smoking. In vain had Travers
begged his wife to go home. She declared that,
having come so far, she would stay and see the last
of us. The brougham had been sent away to a by-
street, as it blocked up the road; so he sat on a
doorstep, she by him on the knapsack. Little
Arthur, who had been delighted at the bustle and
the uniforms, and in high spirits, became at last
very cross, and eventually cried himself to sleep in
his father's arms, his golden hair and one little
dimpled arm hanging over his shoulder. Thus
went on the weary hours, till suddenly the assembly
sounded, and we all started up. We were to
return to Waterloo. The landing on the east was
only a feint—so ran the rumour—the real attack
was on the south. Anything seemed better than
indecision and delay, and, tired though we were,
the march back was gladly hailed. Mrs. Travers,
who made us take the remains of the luncheon

with us, we left to look for her carriage ; little
Arthur, who was awake again, but very good and
quiet, in her arms.

We did not reach Waterloo till nearly midnight,
and there was some delay in starting again.
Several volunteer and militia regiments had
arrived from the north ; the station and all its
approaches were jammed up with men, and trains
were being despatched away as fast as they could
be made-up. All this time no news had reached us
since the first announcement; but the excitement
then aroused had now passed away under the
influence of fatigue and want of sleep, and most of
us dozed off as soon as we got under way. I did,
at any rate, and was awoke by the train stopping
at Leatherhead. There was an up-train returning
to town, and some persons in it were bringing up
news from the coast. We could not, from our part
of the train, hear what they said, but the rumour
was passed up from one carriage to another. The
enemy had landed in force at Worthing. Their
position had been attacked by the troops from the
camp near Brighton, and the action would be
renewed in the morning. The volunteers had
behaved very well. This was all the information
we could get. So, then, the invasion had come at
last. It was clear, at any rate, from what was
said, that the enemy had not been driven back
yet, and we should be in time most likely to take
a share in the defence. It was sunrise when the
train crawled into Dorking, for there had been

numerous stoppages on the way; and here it was
pulled up for a long time, and we were told to get
out and stretch ourselves—an order gladly responded to, for we had been very closely packed all
night. Most of us, too, took the opportunity to
make an early breakfast off the food we had
brought from Shoreditch. I had the remains of
Mrs. Travers's fowl and some bread wrapped up
in my waterproof, which I shared with one or two
less provident comrades. We could see from our
halting-place that the line was blocked with trains
beyond and behind. It must have been about
eight o'clock when we got orders to take our seats
again, and the train began to move slowly on
towards Horsham. Horsham Junction was the
point to be occupied—so the rumour went; but
about ten o'clock, when halting at a small station
a few miles short of it, the order came to leave the
train, and our brigade formed in column on the
high road. Beyond us was some field artillery;
and further on, so we were told by a staff-officer,
another brigade, which was to make up a division
with ours. After more delays the line began to
move, but not forwards; our route was towards
the north-west, and a sort of suspicion of the state
of affairs flashed across my mind. Horsham was
already occupied by the enemy's advance-guard,
and we were to fall back on Leith Common, and
take up a position threatening his flank, should he
advance either to Guildford or Dorking. This
was soon confirmed by what the colonel was told

by the brigadier and passed down the ranks; and
just now, for the first time, the boom of artillery
came up on the light south breeze. In about an
hour the firing ceased. What did it mean? We
could not tell. Meanwhile our march continued.
The day was very close and sultry, and the clouds
of dust stirred up by our feet almost suffocated us.
I had saved a soda-water-bottleful of yesterday's
claret; but this went only a short way, for there
were many mouths to share it with, and the thirst
soon became as bad as ever. Several of the regiment fell out from faintness, and we made frequent
halts to rest and let the stragglers come up. At
last we reached the top of Leith Hill. It is a
striking spot, being the highest point in the south
of England. The view from it is splendid, and
most lovely did the country look this summer day,
although the grass was brown from the long
drought. It was a great relief to get from the
dusty road on to the common, and at the top of
the hill there was a refreshing breeze. We could
see now, for the first time, the whole of our division.
Our own regiment did not muster more than 500,
for it contained a large number of Government
office-men who had been detained, like Danvers,
for duty in town, and others were not much larger;
but the militia regiment was very strong, and the
whole division, I was told, mustered nearly 5,000
rank and file. We could see other troops also in
extension of our division, and could count a
couple of field-batteries of Royal Artillery, besides

some heavy guns, belonging to the volunteers
apparently, drawn by cart-horses. The cooler air,
the sense of numbers, and the evident strength of
the position we held, raised our spirits, which, I
am not ashamed to say, had all the morning been
depressed. It was not that we were not eager to
close with the enemy, but that the counter-march-
ing and halting ominously betokened a vacillation
of purpose in those who had the guidance of affairs.
Here in two days the invaders had got more than
twenty miles inland, and nothing effectual had
been done to stop them. And the ignorance in
which we volunteers, from the colonel downwards,
were kept of their movements, filled us with uneasiness. We could not but depict to ourselves
the enemy as carrying out all the while firmly his
well-considered scheme of attack, and contrasting
it with our own uncertainty of purpose. The very
silence with which his advance appeared to be con-
ducted filled us with mysterious awe. Meanwhile
the day wore on, and we became faint with hunger,
for we had eaten nothing since daybreak. No
provisions came up, and there were no signs of any
commissariat officers. It seems that when we
were at the Waterloo station a whole trainful of
provisions was drawn up there, and our colonel
proposed that one of the trucks should be taken
off and attached to our train, so that we might
have some food at hand ; but the officer in charge
an assistant-controller I think they called him—
this control department was a newfangled affair

which did us almost as much harm as the enemy
in the long-run—said his orders were to keep all the
stores together, and that he couldn't issue any
without authority from the head of his department. So we had to go without. Those who had
tobacco smoked—indeed there is no solace like a
pipe under such circumstances. The militia
regiment, I heard afterwards, had two days' provisions in their haversacks; it was we volunteers
who had no haversacks, and nothing to put in
them. All this time, I should tell you, while we
were lying on the grass with our arms piled, the
General, with the brigadiers and staff, was riding
about slowly from point to point of the edge of the
common, looking out with his glass towards the
south valley. Orderlies and staff-officers were
constantly coming, and about three o'clock there
arrived up a road that led towards Horsham a
small body of lancers and a regiment of yeomanry,
who had, it appears, been out in advance, and now
drew up a short way in front of us in column facing
to the south. Whether they could see anything in
their front I could not tell, for we were behind the
crest of the hill ourselves, and so could not look
into the valley below; but shortly afterwards the
assembly sounded. Commanding officers were
called out by the General, and received some brief
instructions; and the column began to march
again towards London, the militia this time coming last in our brigade. A rumour regarding the
object of this counter-march soon spread through

the ranks. The enemy was not going to attack us
here, but was trying to turn the position on both
sides; one column pointing to Reigate, the other to
Aldershot ; and so we must fall back and take up
a position at Dorking. The line of the great chalk-
range was to be defended. A large force was con-
centrating at Guildford, another at Reigate, and
we should find supports at Dorking. The enemy
would be awaited in these positions. Such, so far
as we privates could get at the facts, was to be the
plan of operations. Down the hill, therefore, we
marched. From one or two points we could catch
a brief sight of the railway in the valley below
running from Dorking to Horsham. Men in red
were working upon it here and there. They were
the Royal Engineers, some one said, breaking up
the line. On we marched. The dust seemed worse
than ever. In one village through which we
passed—I forget the name now—there was a
pump on the green. Here we stopped and had a
good drink ; and passing by a large farm, the
farmer's wife and two or three of her maids stood
at the gate and handed us hunches of bread and
cheese out of some baskets. I got the share of a
bit, but the bottom of the good woman's baskets
must soon have been reached. Not a thing else
was to be had till we got to Dorking about six
o'clock ; indeed most of the farmhouses appeared
deserted already. On arriving there we were
drawn up in the street; and just opposite was a
baker's shop. Our fellows asked leave at first by

twos and threes to go in and buy some loaves, but soon others began to break off and crowd into the shop, and at last a regular scramble took place. If there had been any order preserved, and a regular distribution arranged, they would no doubt have been steady enough, but hunger makes men selfish ; each man felt that his stopping behind would do no good—he would simply lose his share ; so it ended by almost the whole regiment joining in the scrimmage, and the shop was cleared out in a couple of minutes ; while as for paying, you could not get your hand into your pocket for the crush. The colonel tried in vain to stop the row ; some of the officers were as bad as the men. Just then a staff-officer rode by ; he could scarcely make way for the crowd, and was pushed against rather rudely, and in a passion he called out to us to behave properly, like soldiers, and not like a parcel of roughs. "Oh, blow it, governor," said Dick Wake, "you aren't agoing to come between a poor cove and his grub." Wake was an articled attorney, and, as we used to say in those days, a cheeky young chap, although a good-natured fellow enough. At this speech, which was followed by some more remarks of the sort from those about him, the staff-officer became angrier still. "Orderly," cried he to the lancer riding behind him, "take that man to the provost-marshal. As for you, sir," he said, turning to our colonel, who sat on his horse silent with astonishment, "if you don't want some of your men shot before their time, you and your precious officers had better keep this rabble in a little better order"; and poor Dick, who looked crestfallen enough, would certainly have been led off at the tail of the sergeant's horse, if the brigadier had not come up and arranged matters, and marched us off to the hill beyond the town. This incident made us both angry and crestfallen. We were annoyed at being so roughly spoken to: at the same time we felt we had deserved it, and were ashamed of the miscon- duct. Then, too, we had lost confidence in our colonel, after the poor figure he cut in the affair. He was a good fellow, the colonel, and showed himself a brave one next day; but he aimed too much at being popular, and didn't understand a bit how to command.

To resume :—We had scarcely reached the hill above the town, which we were told was to be our bivouac for the night, when the welcome news came that a food-train had arrived at the station; but there were no carts to bring the things up, so a fatigue-party went down and carried back a supply to us in their arms,—loaves, a barrel of rum, packets of tea, and joints of meat—abund- ance for all ; but there was not a kettle or a cook- ing-pot in the regiment, and we could not eat the meat raw. The colonel and officers were no better off. They had arranged to have a regular mess, with crockery, steward, and all complete, but the establishment never turned up, and what had become of it no one knew. Some of us were sent

back into the town to see what we could procure
in the way of cooking utensils. We found the
street full of artillery, baggage-waggons, and
mounted officers, and volunteers shopping like
ourselves; and all the houses appeared to be
occupied by troops. We succeeded in getting a
few kettles and saucepans, and I obtained for
myself a leather bag, with a strap to go over the
shoulder, which proved very handy afterwards;
and thus laden, we trudged back to our camp on
the hill, filling the kettles with dirty water from a
little stream which runs between the hill and the
town, for there was none to be had above. It was
nearly a couple of miles each way; and, exhausted
as we were with marching and want of rest, we
were almost too tired to eat. The cooking was of
the roughest, as you may suppose; all we could
do was to cut off slices of the meat and boil them
in the saucepans, using our fingers for forks. The
tea, however, was very refreshing; and, thirsty as
we were, we drank it by the gallon. Just before it
grew dark, the brigade-major came round, and,
with the adjutant, showed our colonel how to set
a picket in advance of our line a little way down
the face of the hill. It was not necessary to place
one, I suppose, because the town in our front was
still occupied with troops; but no doubt the
practice would be useful. We had also a quarter-
guard, and a line of sentries in front and rear of
our line, communicating with those of the regiments on our flanks. Firewood was plentiful, for

the hill was covered with beautiful wood ; but it took some time to collect it, for we had nothing but our pocket-knives to cut down the branches with.

So we lay down to sleep. My company had no duty, and we had the night undisturbed to ourselves ; but, tired though-I was, the excitement and the novelty of the situation made sleep difficult. And although the night was still and warm, and we were sheltered by the woods, I soon found it chilly with no better covering than my thin dust-coat, the more so as my clothes, saturated with perspiration during the day, had never dried ; and before daylight I woke from a short nap, shivering with cold, and was glad to get warm with others by a fire. I then noticed that the opposite hills on the south were dotted with fires ; and we thought at first they must belong to the enemy, but we were told that the ground up there was still held by a strong rear-guard of regulars, and that there need be no fear of a surprise.

At the first sign of dawn the bugles of the regiments sounded the *reveillé,* and we were ordered to fall in, and the roll was called. About twenty men were absent, who had fallen out sick the day before ; they had been sent up to London by train during the night, I believe. After standing in column for about half an hour, the brigade-major came down with orders to pile arms and stand easy ; and perhaps half an hour afterwards we were told to get breakfast as quickly as possible,

D

and to cook a day's food at the same time. This
operation was managed pretty much in the same
way as the evening before, except that we had our
cooking-pots and kettles ready. Meantime there
was leisure to look around, and from where we
stood there was a commanding view of one of the
most beautiful scenes in England. Our regiment
was drawn up on the extremity of the ridge which
runs from Guildford to Dorking. This is indeed
merely a part of the great chalk-range which extends from beyond Aldershot east to the Medway ;
but there is a gap in the ridge just here where the
little stream that runs past Dorking turns suddenly
to the north, to find its way to the Thames. We
stood on the slope of the hill, as it trends down
eastward towards this gap, and had passed our
bivouac in what appeared to be a gentleman's
park. A little way above us, and to our right, was
a very fine country-seat to which the park was
attached, now occupied by the headquarters of
our division. From this house the hill sloped
steeply down southward to the valley below,
which runs nearly east and west parallel to the
ridge, and carries the railway and the road from
Guildford to Reigate ; and in which valley, immediately in front of the chateau, and perhaps a
mile and a half distant from it, was the little town
of Dorking, nestled in the trees, and rising up the
foot of the slopes on the other side of the valley
which stretched away to Leith Common, the scene
of yesterday's march. Thus the main part of the

town of Dorking was on our right front, but the suburbs stretched away eastward nearly to our proper front, culminating in a small railway station, from which the grassy slopes of the park rose up dotted with shrubs and trees to where we were standing. Round this railway station was a cluster of villas and one or two mills, of whose gardens we thus had a bird's-eye view, their little ornamental ponds glistening like looking-glasses in the morning sun. Immediately on our left the park sloped steeply down to the gap before mentioned, through which ran the little stream, as well as the railway from Epsom to Brighton, nearly due north and south, meeting the Guildford and Reigate line at right angles. Close to the point of intersection and the little station already mentioned, was the station of the former line where we had stopped the day before. Beyond the gap on the east (our left), and in continuation of our ridge, rose the chalk-hill again. The shoulder of this ridge overlooking the gap is called Box Hill, from the shrubbery of boxwood with which it was covered. Its sides were very steep, and the top of the ridge was covered with troops. The natural strength of our position was manifested at a glance, a high grassy ridge steep to the south, with a stream in front, and but little cover up the sides. It seemed made for a battle-field. The weak point was the gap; the ground at the junction of the railways and the roads immediately at the entrance of the gap formed a little valley, dotted, as I have

said, with buildings and gardens. This, in one
sense, was the key of the position; for although it
would not be tenable while we held the ridge commanding it, the enemy by carrying this point and
advancing through the gap would cut our line in
two. But you must not suppose I scanned the
ground thus critically at the time. Anybody,
indeed, might have been struck with the natural
advantages of our position; but what, as I
remember, most impressed me, was the peaceful
beauty of the scene—the little town with the
outline of the houses obscured by a blue mist, the
massive crispness of the foliage, the outlines of the
great trees, lighted up by the sun, and relieved by
deep-blue shade. So thick was the timber here,
rising up the southern slopes of the valley, that it
looked almost as if it might have been a primeval
forest. The quiet of the scene was the more im-
pressive because contrasted in the mind with the
scenes we expected to follow; and I can remember
as if it were yesterday, the sensation of bitter
regret that it should now be too late to avert this
coming desecration of our country, which might
so easily have been prevented. A little firmness,
a little prevision on the part of our rulers, even a
little common sense, and this great calamity
would have been rendered utterly impossible. Too
late, alas! We were like the foolish virgins in the
parable.

But you must not suppose the scene immediately
around was gloomy: the camp was brisk and

bustling enough. We had got over the stress of weariness; our stomachs were full; we felt a natural enthusiasm at the prospect of having so soon to take a part as the real defenders of the country, and we were inspirited at the sight of the large force that was now assembled. Along the slopes which trended off to the rear of our ridge, troops came marching up—volunteers, militia, cavalry, and guns; these, I heard, had come down from the north as far as Leatherhead the night before, and had marched over at daybreak. Long trains, too, began to arrive by the rail through the gap, one after the other, containing militia, and volunteers, who moved up to the ridge to the right and left, and took up their position, massed for the most part on the slopes which ran up from, and in rear of, where we stood. We now formed part of an army corps, we were told, consisting of three divisions, but what regiments composed the other two divisions I never heard. All this movement we could distinctly see from our position, for we had hurried over our breakfast, expecting every minute that the battle would begin, and now stood or sat about on the ground near our piled arms. Early in the morning, too, we saw a very long train come along the valley from the direction of Guildford, full of redcoats. It halted at the little station at our feet, and the troops alighted. We could soon make out their bear-skins. They were the Guards, coming to reinforce this part of the line. Leaving a detachment of skirmishers to hold the

line of the railway embankment, the main body
marched up with a springy step and with the band
playing, and drew up across the gap on our left, in
prolongation of our line. There appeared to be
three battalions of them, for they formed up in
that number of columns at short intervals.

Shortly after this I was sent over to Box Hill
with a message from our colonel to the colonel of
a volunteer regiment stationed there, to know
whether an ambulance-cart was obtainable, as it
was reported this regiment was well supplied with
carriage, whereas we were without any : my mis-
sion, however, was futile. Crossing the valley, I
found a scene of great confusion at the railway
station. Trains were still coming in with stores,
ammunition, guns, and appliances of all sorts,
which were being unloaded as fast as possible ;
but there were scarcely any means of getting the
things off. There were plenty of waggons of all
sorts, but hardly any horses to draw them, and
the whole place was blocked up ; while, to add to
the confusion, a regular exodus had taken place of
the people from the town, who had been warned
that it was likely to be the scene of fighting.
Ladies and women of all sorts and ages, and children, some with bundles, some empty-handed,
were seeking places in the train, but there appeared no one on the the spot authorized to grant
them, and these poor creatures were pushing their
way up and down, vainly asking for information
and permission to get away. In the crowd I

observed our surgeon, who likewise was in search
of an ambulance of some sort : his whole profes-
sional apparatus, he said, consisted of a case of
instruments. Also in the crowd I stumbled upon
Wood, Travers's old coachman. He had been
send down by his mistress to Guildford, because it
was supposed our regiment had gone there, riding
the horse, and laden with a supply of things—
food, blankets, and, of course, a letter. He had
also brought my knapsack; but at Guildford the
horse was pressed for artillery work, and a receipt
for it given him in exchange, so he had been
obliged to leave all the heavy packages there, including my knapsack; but the faithful old man
had brought on as many things as he could carry,
and hearing that we should be found in this part,
had walked over thus laden from Guildford.
He said that place was crowded with troops, and
that the heights were lined with them the whole
way between the two towns; also, that some
trains with wounded had passed up from the coast
in the night, through Guildford. I led him off to
where our regiment was, relieving the old man
from part of the load he was staggering under.
The food sent was not now so much needed, but
the plates, knives, etc., and drinking-vessels,
promised to be handy—and Travers, you may be
sure, was delighted to get his letter; while a
couple of newspapers the old man had brought
were eagerly competed for by all, even at this
critical moment, for we had heard no authentic

news since we left London on Sunday. And even
at this distance of time, although I only glanced
down the paper, I can remember almost the very
words I read there. They were both copies of the
same paper : the first, published on Sunday evening, when the news had arrived of the successful
landing at three points, was written in a tone of
despair. The country must confess that it had
been taken by surprise. The conqueror would be
satisfied with the humiliation inflicted by a peace
dictated on our own shores ; it was the clear duty
of the Government to accept the best terms obtainable, and to avoid further bloodshed and disaster, and avert the fall of our tottering mercan-
tile credit. The next morning's issue was in quite
a different tone. Apparently the enemy had received a check, for we were here exhorted to
resistance. An impregnable position was to be
taken up along the Downs, a force was concen-
trating there far outnumbering the rash invaders,
who, with an invincible line before them, and the
sea behind, had no choice between destruction or
surrender. Let there be no pusillanimous talk of
negotiation, the fight must be fought out ; and
there could be but one issue. England, expectant
but calm, awaited with confidence the result of the
attack on its unconquerable volunteers. The
writing appeared to me eloquent, but rather in-
consistent. The same paper said the Government
had sent off 500 workmen from Woolwich, to open
a branch arsenal at Birmingham.

All this time we had nothing to do, except to change our position, which we did every few minutes, now moving up the h'll farther to our right, now taking ground lower down to our left, as one order after another was brought down the line ; but the staff-officers were galloping about perpetually with orders, while the rumble of the artillery as they moved about from one part of the field to another went on almost incessantly. At last the whole line stood to arms, the bands struck up, and the General commanding our army corps came riding down with his staff. We had seen him several times before, as we had been moving frequently about the position during the morning ; but he now made a sort of formal inspection. He was a tall thin man, with long light hair, very well mounted, and as he sat his horse with an erect seat, and came prancing down the line, at a little distance he looked as if he might be five-and-twenty ; but I believe he had served more than fifty years, and had been made a peer for services performed when quite an old man. I remember that he had more decorations than there was room for on the breast of his coat, and wore them suspended like a necklace round his neck. Like all the other generals, he was dressed in blue, with a cocked-hat and feathers—a bad plan, I thought, for it made them very conspicuous: The general halted before our battalion, and after looking at us a while, made a short address: We had a post of honour next Her Majesty's Guards, and would show our-

selves worthy of it, and of the name of Englishmen. It did not need, he said, to be a general to
see the strength of our position; it was impregnable, if properly held. Let us wait till the enemy
was well pounded, and then the word would be
given to go at him. Above everything, we must
be steady. He then shook hands with our colonel,
we gave him a cheer, and he rode on to where the
Guards were drawn up.

Now then, we thought, the battle will begin.
But still there were no signs of the enemy; and
the air, though hot and sultry, began to be very
hazy, so that you could scarcely see the town
below, and the hills opposite were merely a confused blur, in which no features could be distinctly made out. After a while, the tension of
feeling which followed the General's address re-
laxed, and we began to feel less as if everything
depended on keeping our rifles firmly grasped:
we were told to pile arms again, and got leave to
go down by tens and twenties to the stream below
to drink. This stream, and all the hedges and
banks on our side of it, were held by our skirmishers, but the town had been abandoned. The
position appeared an excellent one; except that
the enemy, when they came, would have almost
better cover than our men. While I was down at
the brook, a column emerged from the town,
making for our position. We thought for a
moment it was the enemy, and you could not
make out the colour of the uniforms for the dust;

but it turned out to be our rear-guard, falling back
from the opposite hills which they had occupied
the previous night. One battalion, of rifles,
halted for a few minutes at the stream to let the
men drink, and I had a minute's talk with a
couple of the officers. They had formed part of
the force which had attacked the enemy on their
first landing. They had it all their own way, they
said, at first, and could have beaten the enemy
back easily if they had been properly supported;
but the whole thing was mismanaged. The volunteers came on very pluckily, they said, but they
got into confusion, and so did the militia, and the
attack failed, with serious loss. It was the
wounded of this force which had passed through
Guildford in the night. The officers asked us
eagerly about the arrangements for the battle,
and when we said that the Guards were the only
regular troops in this part of the field, shook their
heads ominously.

While we were talking a third officer came up;
he was a dark man with a smooth face and a
curious excited manner. "You are volunteers, I
suppose," he said; quickly, his eye flashing the
while. "Well, now, look here; mind I don't
want to hurt your feelings, or to say anything un-
pleasant, but I'll tell you what; if all you gentlemen were just to go back, and leave us to fight it
out alone, it would be a devilish good thing. We
could do it a precious deal better without you, I
assure you. We don't want your help; I can tell

you. We would much rather be left alone, I
assure you. Mind I don't want to say anything
rude, but that's a fact." Having blurted out this
passionately, he strode away before any one could
reply, or the other officers could stop him. They
apologized for his rudeness, saying that his
brother, also in the regiment, had been killed on
Sunday, and that this, and the sun, and marching,
had affected his head. The officers told us that
the enemy's advanced-guard was close behind,
but that he had apparently been waiting for re-
inforcements, and would probably not attack in
force until noon. It was, however, nearly three
o'clock before the battle began. We had almost
worn out the feeling of expectancy. For twelve
hours had we been waiting for the coming struggle, till at last it seemed almost as if the invasion
were but a bad dream, and the enemy, as yet unseen by us, had no real existence. So far things
had not been very different, but for the numbers
and for what we had been told, from a Volunteer
review on Brighton Downs. I remember that these
thoughts were passing through my mind as we lay
down in groups on the grass, some smoking, some
nibbling at their bread, some even asleep, when
the listless state we had fallen into was suddenly
disturbed by a gunshot fired from the top of the
hill on our right, close by the big house. It was the
first time I had ever heard a shotted gun fired, and
although it is fifty years ago, the angry whistle
of the shot as it left the gun is in my ears now. The

sound was soon to become common enough. We
all jumped up at the report, and fell in almost with
out the word being-given, grasping our rifles
tightly, and the leading files peering forward to
look for the approaching enemy. This gun was
apparently the signal to begin, for now our batteries opened fire all along the line. What they
were firing at I could not see, and I am sure the
gunners could not see much themselves. I have
told you what a haze had come over the air since
the morning, and now the smoke from the guns
settled like a pall over the hill, and soon we could
see little but the men in our ranks, and the outline
of some gunners in the battery drawn up next us
on the slope on our right. This firing went on, I
should think, for nearly a couple of hours, and still
there was no reply. We could see the gunners—it
was a troop of horse-artillery—working away like
fury, ramming, loading, and running up with cartridges, the officer in command riding slowly up
and down just behind his guns, and peering out
with his field-glasses into the mist. Once or twice
they ceased firing to let their smoke clear away,
but this did not do much good. For nearly two
hours did this go on, and not a shot came in reply.
"If a battle is like this," said Dick Wake, who was
my next-hand file, "it's mild work, to say the least."
The words were hardly uttered when a rattle of
musketry was heard in front; our skirmishers
were at it, and very soon the bullets began to sing
over our heads, and some struck the ground at our

feet. Up to this time we had been in column; we were now deployed into line on the ground assigned to us. From the valley or gap on our left there ran a lane right up the hill almost due west, or along our front. This lane had a thick bank about four feet high, and the greater part of the regiment was drawn up behind it; but a little way up the hill the lane trended back out of the line, so the right of the regiment here left it and occupied the open grass-land of the park. The bank had been cut away at this point to admit of our going in and out. We had been told in the morning to cut down the bushes on the top of the bank, so as to make the space clear for firing over, but we had no tools to work with; however, a party of sappers had come down and finished the job. My company was on the right, and was thus beyond the shelter of the friendly bank. On our right again was the battery of artillery already mentioned; then came a battalion of the line, then more guns, then a great mass of militia and volunteers and a few line up to the big house. At least this was the order before the firing began; after that I do not know what changes took place.

And now the enemy's artillery began to open; where their guns were posted we could not see; but we began to hear the rush of the shells over our heads, and the bang as they burst just beyond. And now what took place I can really hardly tell you. Sometimes when I try and recall the scene, it seems as if it lasted for only a few minutes; yet I

know; as we lay on the ground, I thought the
hours would never pass away, as we watched the
gunners still plying their task, firing at the invis-
ible enemy, never stopping for a moment except
when now and again a dull blow would be heard
and a man fall down, then three or four of his
comrades would carry him to the rear. The captain no longer rode up and down; what had become of him, I do not know. Two of the guns
ceased firing for a time; they had got injured in
some way, and up rode an artillery general. I
think I see him now, a very handsome man, with
straight features and a dark moustache, his breast
covered with medals. He appeared in a great
rage at the guns stopping fire.

" Who commands this battery ? " he cried.

" I do, Sir Henry," said an officer, riding forward, whom I had not noticed before.

The group is before me at this moment, standing out clear against the background of smoke,
Sir Henry erect on his splendid charger, his
flashing eye, his left arm pointing towards the
enemy to enforce something he was going to say,
the young officer reining in his horse just beside
him, and saluting with his right hand raised to his
busby. This for a moment, then a dull thud, and
both horses and riders are prostrate on the ground.
A round-shot had struck all four at the saddle-
line. Some of the gunners ran up to help, but
neither officer could have lived many minutes.
This was not the first I saw killed. Some time

before this, almost immediately on the enemy's artillery opening, as we were lying, I heard something
like the sound of metal striking metal, and at the
same moment Dick Wake, who was next me in the
ranks, leaning on his elbows, sank forward on his
face. I looked round and saw what had happened;
a shot fired at a high elevation, passing over his
head, had struck the ground behind, nearly cutting his thigh off. It must have been the ball
striking his sheathed bayonet which made the
noise. Three of us carried the poor fellow to the
rear, with difficulty for the shattered limb; but
he was nearly dead from loss of blood when we got
to the doctor, who was waiting in a sheltered hollow about two hundred yards in rear, with two
other doctors in plain clothes, who had come up to
help. We deposited our burden and returned to the
front. Poor Wake was sensible when we left him,
but apparently too shaken by the shock to be able
to speak. Wood was there helping the doctors.
I paid more visits to the rear of the same sort
before the evening was over.

All this time we were lying there to be fired at
without returning a shot, for our skirmishers were
holding the line of walls and enclosures below.
However, the bank protected most of us, and the
brigadier now ordered our right company, which
was in the open, to get behind it also; and there
we lay about four deep, the shells crashing and
bullets whistling over our heads, but hardly a man
being touched. Our colonel was, indeed, the only

one exposed, for he rode up and down the lane at
a foot-pace as steady as a rock ; but he made the
major and adjutant dismount, and take shelter
behind the hedge; holding their horses. We were
all pleased to see him so cool, and it restored our
confidence in him, which had been shaken yesterday.

The time seemed interminable while we lay thus
inactive. We could not, of course, help peering
over the bank to try and see what was going on ;
but there was nothing to be made out, for now a
tremendous thunder-storm, which had been gath-
ering all day, burst on us, and a torrent of almost
blinding rain came down, which obscured the view
even more than the smoke, while the crashing of
the thunder and the glare of the lightning could
be heard and seen seen even above the roar and
flashing of the artillery. Once the mist lifted,
and I saw for a minute an attack on Box Hill, on
the other side of the gap on our left. It was like
the scene at a theatre—a curtain of smoke all
round and a clear gap in the centre, with a sudden
gleam of evening sunshine lighting it up. The
steep smooth slope of the hill was crowded with the
dark-blue figures of the enemy, whom I now saw
for the first time—an irregular outline in front,
but very solid in rear : the whole body was
moving forward by fits and starts, the men firing
and advancing, the officers waving their swords,
the columns closing up and gradually making way.
Our people were almost concealed by the bushes

E

at the top, whence the smoke and their fire could
be seen proceeding : presently from these bushes
on the crest came out a red line; and dashed down
the brow of the hill, a flame of fire belching out
from the front as it advanced. The enemy hesi-
tated, gave way, and finally ran back in a confused crowd down the hill. Then the mist covered the scene, but the glimpse of this splendid
charge was inspiriting, and I hoped we should
show the same coolness when it came to our turn.
It was about this time that our skirmishers fell
back, a good many wounded, some limping along
by themselves, others helped. The main body
retired in very fair order, halting to turn round
and fire ; we could see a mounted officer of the
Guards riding up and down encouraging them to
be steady. Now came our turn. For a few
minutes we saw nothing, but a rattle of bullets
came through the rain and mist, mostly, however,
passing over the bank. We began to fire in reply,
stepping up against the bank to fire, and stooping
down to load ; but our brigade-major rode up
with an order, and the word was passed through
the men to reserve our fire. In a very few moments it must have been that, when ordered to
stand up, we could see the helmet-spikes and then
the figures of the skirmishers as they came on :
a lot of them there appeared to be, five or six deep
I should say, but in loose order, each man stopping
to aim and fire, and then coming forward a little.
Just then the brigadier clattered on horseback up

the lane. "Now then, gentlemen, give it them
hot!" he cried; and fire away we did, as fast as
ever we were able. perfect storm of bullets
seemed to be flying about us too, and I thought
each moment must be the last; escape seemed
impossible, but I saw no one fall, for I was too
busy, and so were we all, to look to the right or
left, but loaded and fired as fast as we could. How
long this went on I know not—it could not have
been long; neither side could have lasted many
minutes under such a fire, but it ended by the
enemy gradually falling back, and as soon as we
saw this we raised a tremendous shout, and some
of us jumped up on the bank to give them our
parting shots. Suddenly the order was passed
down the line to cease firing, and we soon dis-
covered the cause; a battalion of the Guards was
charging obliquely across from our left across our
front. It was, I expect, their flank attack as much
as our fire which had turned back the enemy; and
it was a splendid sight to see their steady line as
they advanced slowly across the smooth lawn
below us, firing as they went, but as steady as if on
parade. We felt a great elation at this moment;
it seemed as if the battle was won. Just then
somebody called out to look to the wounded, and
for the first time I turned to glance down the rank
along the lane. Then I saw that we had not beaten back the attack without loss. Immediately
before me lay Bob Lawford of my office; dead on
his back from a bullet through his forehead, his

hand still grasping his rifle. At every step was
some friend or acquaintance killed or wounded,
and a few paces down the lane I found Travers,
sitting with his back against the bank. A ball had
gone through his lungs, and blood was coming
from his mouth. I was lifting him up, but the cry
of agony he gave stopped me. I then saw that
this was not his only wound; his thigh was
smashed by a bullet (which must have hit him
when standing on the bank), and the blood streaming down mixed in a muddy puddle with the rain-
water under him. Still he could not be left here,
so, lifting him up as well as I could, I carried him
through the gate which led out of the lane at the
back to where our camp hospital was in the rear.
The movement must have caused him awful
agony, for I could not support the broken thigh,
and he could not restrain his groans, brave fellow
though he was ; but how I carried him at all I
cannot make out, for he was a much bigger man
than myself ; but I had not gone far, one of a
stream of our fellows, all on the same errand, when
a bandsman and Wood met me, bringing a hurdle
as a stretcher, and on this we placed him. Wood
had just time to tell me that he had got a cart
down in the hollow, and would endeavour to take
off his master at once to Kingston, when a staff-
officer rode up to call us to the ranks. "You
really must not straggle in this way, gentlemen,"
he said ; "pray keep your ranks." " But we
can't leave our wounded to be trodden down and

die," cried one of our fellows. "Beat off the enemy first, sir," he replied. "Gentlemen, do, pray,
join your regiments, or we shall be a regular mob."
And no doubt he did not speak too soon; for
besides our fellows straggling to the rear, lots of
volunteers from the regiments in reserve were
running forward to help, till the whole ground was
dotted with groups of men. I hastened back to
my post, but I had just time to notice that all the
ground in our rear was occupied by a thick mass
of troops, much more numerous than in the
morning, and a column was moving down to the
left of our line, to the ground before held by the
Guards. All this time, although musketry had
slackened, the artillery-fire seemed heavier than
ever; the shells screamed overhead or burst
around; and I confess to feeling quite a relief at
getting back to the friendly shelter of the lane.
Looking over the bank, I noticed for the first time
the frightful execution our fire had created. The
space in front was thickly strewed with dead and
badly wounded, and beyond the bodies of the
fallen enemy could just be seen—for it was now
getting dusk—the bear-skins and red coats of our
own gallant Guards scattered over the slope, and
marking the line of their victorious advance. But
hardly a minute could have passed in thus looking
over the field, when our brigade-major came
moving up the lane on foot (I suppose his horse
had been shot), crying, "Stand to your arms,
volunteers! they're coming on again;" and we

found ourselves a second time engaged in a hot
musketry-fire. How long it went on I cannot now
remember, but we could distinguish clearly the
thick line of skirmishers, about sixty paces off
and mounted officers among them; and we seemed
to be keeping them well in check, for they were
quite exposed to our fire, while we were protected
nearly up to our shoulders, when—I know not
how—I became sensible that something had gone
wrong. "We are taken in flank!" called out
some one; and looking along the left, sure enough
there were dark figures jumping over the bank into
the lane and firing up along our line. The volunteers in reserve, who had come down to take the
place of the Guards, must have given way at this
point; the enemy's skirmishers had got through
our line, and turned our left flank. How the next
move came about I cannot recollect, or whether it
was without orders, but in a short time we found
ourselves out of the lane, and drawn-up in a straggling line about thirty yards in rear of it—at our
end, that is, the other flank had fallen back a good
deal more—and the enemy were lining the hedge,
and numbers of them passing over and forming
up on our side. Beyond our left a confused mass
were retreating, firing as they went, followed by
the advancing line of the enemy. We stood in this
way for a short space, firing at random as fast as
we could. Our colonel and major must have been
shot, for there was no one to give an order, when
somebody on horseback called out from behind—

I think it must have been the brigadier—" Now,
then, volunteers! give a British cheer, and go at
them—charge! " and, with a shout, we rushed at
the enemy. Some of them ran, some stopped to
meet us, and for a moment it was a real hand-to-
hand fight. I felt a sharp sting in my leg, as I
drove my bayonet right through the man in front
of me. I confess I shut my eyes, for I just got a
glimpse of the poor wretch as he fell back, his eyes
starting out of his head, and, savage though we
were, the sight was almost too horrible to look at.
But the struggle was over in a second, and we had
cleared the ground again right up to the rear
hedge of the lane. Had we gone on, I believe we
might have recovered the lane too, but we were
now all out of order; there was no one to say what
to do; the enemy began to line the hedge and
open fire, and they were streaming past our left;
and how it came about I know not, but we found
ourselves falling back towards our right rear,
scarce any semblance of a line remaining, and the
volunteers who had given way on our left mixed
up with us, and adding to the confusion. It was
now nearly dark. On the slopes which we were
retreating to was a large mass of reserves drawn
up in columns. Some of the leading files of these,
mistaking us for the enemy, began firing at us;
our fellows, crying out to them to stop, ran towards their ranks, and in a few moments the whole
slope of the hill became a scene of confusion that
I cannot attempt to describe, regiments and de-

tachments mixed up in hopeless disorder. Most
of us, I believe, turned towards the enemy and
fired away our few remaining cartridges; but it
was too late to take aim, fortunately for us, or
the guns which the enemy had brought up through
the gap, and were firing point-blank, would have
done more damage. As it was, we could see little
more than the bright flashes of their fire. In our
confusion we had jammed up a line regiment immediately behind us, which I suppose had just
arrived on the field, and its colonel and some staff-
officers were in vain trying to make a passage for
it, and their shouts to us to march to the rear and
clear a road could be heard above the roar of the
guns and the confused babel of sound. At last a
mounted officer pushed his way through, followed
by a company in sections, the men brushing past
with firm-set faces, as if on a desperate task; and
the battalion, when it got clear, appeared to de-
ploy and advance down the slope. I have also a
dim recollection of seeing the Life Guards trot
past the front, and push on towards the town—a
last desperate attempt to save the day—before
we left the field. Our adjutant, who had got separated from our flank of the regiment in the confusion, now came up, and managed to lead us, or
at any rate some of us, up to the crest of the hill
in the rear, to re-form, as he said; but there we
met a vast crowd of volunteers, militia, and waggons, all hurrying rearward from the direction of
the big house, and we were borne in the stream for

a mile at least before it was possible to stop. At
last the adjutant led us to an open space a little
off the line of fugitives, and there we re-formed
the remains of the companies. Telling us to halt,
he rode off to try and obtain orders, and find out
where the rest of our brigade was. From this
point, a spur of high ground running off from the
main plateau, we looked down through the dim
twilight into the battle-field below. Artillery-fire
was still going on. We could see the flashes from
the guns on both sides, and now and then a stray
shell came screaming up and burst near us, but we
were beyond the sound of musketry. This halt
first gave us time to think about what had happened. The long day of expectancy had been succeeded by the excitement of battle; and when
each minute may be your last, you do not think
much about other people, nor when you are facing
another man with a rifle have you time to consider
whether he or you are the invader, or that you are
fighting for your home and hearths. All fighting
is pretty much alike, I suspect, as to sentiment,
when once it begins. But now we had time for
reflection; and although we did not yet quite
understand how far the day had gone against us,
an uneasy feeling of self-condemnation must have
come up in the minds of most of us; while, above
all, we now began to realise what the loss of this
battle meant to the country. Then, too, we knew
not what had become of all our wounded comrades.
Reaction, too, set in after the fatigue and excite-

ment. For myself, I had found out for the first
time that besides the bayonet-wound in my leg,
a bullet had gone through my left arm, just below
the shoulder, and outside the bone. I remember
feeling something like a blow just when we lost
the lane, but the wound passed unnoticed till
now, when the bleeding had stopped and the shirt
was sticking to the wound.

This half-hour seemed an age, and while we
stood on this knoll the endless tramp of men and
rumbling of carts along the downs beside us told
their own tale. The whole army was falling back.
At last we could discern the adjutant riding up to
us out of the dark. The army was to retreat and
take up a position on Epsom Downs, he said;
we should join in the march, and try and find our
brigade in the morning; and so we turned into
the throng again, and made our way on as best we
could. A few scraps of news he gave us as he rode
alongside of our leading section; the army had
held its position well for a time, but the enemy
had at last broken through the line between us
and Guildford, as well as in our front, and had
poured his men through the point gained, throw-
ing the line into confusion, and the first army
corps near Guildford were also falling back to
avoid being out-flanked. The regular troops were
holding the rear; we were to push on as fast as
possible to get out of their way, and allow them
to make an orderly retreat in the morning. The
gallant old lord commanding our corps had been

badly wounded early in the day, he heard, and
carried off the field. The Guards had suffered
dreadfully; the household cavalry had ridden
down the cuirassiers, but had got into broken
ground and been awfully cut up. Such were the
scraps of news passed down our weary column.
What had become of our wounded no one knew,
and no one liked to ask. So we trudged on. It
must have been midnight when we reached
Leatherhead. Here we left the open ground and
took to the road, and the block became greater.
We pushed our way painfully along; several trains
passed slowly ahead along the railway by the
roadside, containing the wounded, we supposed—
such of them, at least, as were lucky enough to be
picked up. It was daylight when we got to Epsom. The night had been bright and clear after
the storm, with a cool air, which, blowing through
my soaking clothes, chilled me to the bone. My
wounded leg was stiff and sore, and I was ready
to drop with exhaustion and hunger. Nor were
my comrades in much better case ; we had eaten
nothing since breakfast the day before, and the
bread we had put by had been washed away by the
storm : only a little pulp remained at the bottom
of my bag. The tobacco was all too wet to smoke.
In this plight we were creeping along, when the
adjutant guided us into a field by the roadside to
rest awhile, and we lay down exhausted on the
sloppy grass. The roll was here taken, and only
180 answered out of nearly 500 present on the

morning of the battle. How many of these were
killed and wounded no one could tell; but it was
certain many must have got separated in the confusion of the evening. While resting here, we saw
pass by, in the crowd of vehicles and men, a cart
laden with commissariat stores, driven by a man
in uniform. "Food!" cried some one, and a
dozen volunteers jumped up and surrounded the
cart. The driver tried to whip them off; but he
was pulled off his seat, and the contents of the
cart thrown out in an instant. They were preserved meats in tins, which we tore open with our
bayonets. The meat had been cooked before, I
think; at any rate we devoured it. Shortly after
this a general came by with three or four staff-
officers. He stopped and spoke to our adjutant,
and then rode into the field. "My lads," said he,
" you shall join my division for the present: fall
in, and follow the regiment that is now passing."
We rose up, fell in by companies, each about
twenty strong, and turned once more into the
stream moving along the road ;—regiments, detachments, single volunteers or militiamen, country people making off, some with bundles, some
without, a few in carts, but most on foot; here and
there waggons of stores, with men sitting where-
ever there was room, others crammed with wounded soldiers. Many blocks occurred from horses
falling, or carts breaking down and filling up the
road. In the town the confusion was even worse,
for all the houses seemed full of volunteers and

militiamen, wounded, or resting, or trying to find
food, and the streets were almost choked up.
Some officers were in vain trying to restore order,
but the task seemed a hopeless one. One or two
volunteer regiments which had arrived from the
north the previous night, and had been halted
here for orders, were drawn up along the roadside
steadily enough, and some of the retreating regiments, including ours, may have preserved the
semblance of discipline, but for the most part the
mass pushing to the rear was a mere mob. The
regulars, or what remained of them, were now, I
believe, all in the rear, to hold the advancing
enemy in check. A few officers among such a
crowd could do nothing. To add to the confusion
several houses were being emptied of the wounded
brought here the night before, to prevent their
falling into the hands of the enemy, some in carts,
some being carried to the railway by men. The
groans of these poor fellows as they were jostled
through the street went to our hearts, selfish
though fatigue and suffering had made us. At
last, following the guidance of a staff-officer who
was standing to show the way, we turned off from
the main London road and took that towards
Kingston. Here the crush was less, and we managed to move along pretty steadily. The air had
been cooled by the storm, and there was no dust.
We passed through a village where our new general had seized all the public-houses, and taken
possession of the liquor; and each regiment as it

came up was halted, and each man got a drink of
beer, served out by companies. Whether the
owner got paid, I know not, but it was like nectar.
It must have been about one o'clock in the afternoon that we came in sight of Kingston. We had
been on our legs sixteen hours, and had got over
about twelve miles of ground. There is a hill a
little south of the Surbiton station, covered then
mostly with villas, but open at the western extremity, where there was a clump of trees on the
summit. We had diverged from the road towards
this, and here the general halted us and disposed
the line of the division along his front, facing to
the south-west, the right of the line reaching down
to the water-works on the Thames, the left ex-
tending along the southern slope of the hill, in the
direction of the Epsom road by which we had
come. We were nearly in the centre, occupying the
knoll just in front of the general, who dismounted
on the top and tied his horse to a tree. It is not
much of a hill, but commands an extensive view
over the flat country around ; and as we lay
wearily on the ground we could see the Thames
glistening like a silver field in the bright sunshine,
the palace at Hampton Court, the bridge at
Kingston, and the old church tower rising above
the haze of the town, with the woods of Richmond
Park behind it. To most of us the scene could not
but call up the associations of happy days of
peace—days now ended and peace destroyed
through national infatuation. We did not say

this to each other, but a deep depression had come upon us, partly due to weakness and fatigue, no doubt; but we saw that another stand was going to be made, and we had no longer any confidence in ourselves. If we could not hold our own when stationary in line, on a good position, but had been broken up into a rabble at the first shock, what chance had we now of manœuvring against a victorious enemy in this open ground? A feeling of desperation came over us, a determination to struggle on against hope; but anxiety for the future of the country, and our friends, and all dear to us, filled our thoughts now that we had time for reflection. We had had no news of any kind since Wood joined us the day before—we knew not what was doing in London, or what the Government was about, or anything else; and exhausted though we were, we felt an intense craving to know what was happening in other parts of the country.

Our general had expected to find a supply of food and ammunition here, but nothing turned up. Most of us had hardly a cartridge left, so he ordered the regiment next to us, which came from the north and had not been engaged, to give us enough to make up twenty rounds a man, and he sent off a fatigue-party to Kingston to try and get provisions, while a detachment of our fellows was allowed to go foraging among the villas in our rear; and in about an hour they brought back some bread and meat, which gave us a slender

meal all round. They said most of the houses
were empty, and that many had been stripped of
all eatables, and a good deal damaged already.

It must have been between three and four o'clock,
when the sound of cannonading began to be heard
in the front, and we could see the smoke of the
guns rising above the woods of Esher and Clare-
mont, and soon afterwards some troops emerged
from the fields below us. It was the rear-guard of
regular troops. There were some guns also, which
were driven up the slope and took up their position
round the knoll. There were three batteries, but
they only counted eight guns amongst them.
Behind them was posted the line; it was a brigade
apparently of four regiments, but the whole did
not look to be more than eight or nine hundred men.
Our regiment and another had been moved a little
to the rear to make way for them, and presently
we were ordered down to occupy the railway
station on our right rear. My leg was now so stiff
I could no longer march with the rest, and my left
arm was very swollen and sore, and almost useless;
but anything seemed better than being left behind,
so I limped after the battalion as best I could
down to the station. There was a goods shed a
little in advance of it down the line, a strong brick
building, and here my company was posted. The
rest of our men lined the wall of the enclosure. A
staff-officer came with us to arrange the distribution; we should be supported by line troops, he
said; and in a few minutes a train full of them

came slowly up from Guildford way. It was the last; the men got out, the train passed on, and a party began to tear up the rails, while the rest were distributed among the houses on each side. A sergeant's party joined us in our shed, and an engineer officer with sappers came to knock holes in the walls for us to fire from; but there were only half-a-dozen of them, so progress was not rapid, and as we had no tools we could not help.

It was while we were watching this job that the adjutant, who was as active as ever, looked in, and told us to muster in the yard. The fatigue-party had come back from Kingston, and a small baker's hand-cart of food was made over to us as our share. It contained loaves, flour, and some joints of meat. The meat and the flour we had not time or means to cook. The loaves we devoured; and there was a tap of water in the yard, so we felt refreshed by the meal. I should have liked to wash my wounds, which were becoming very offensive, but I dared not take off my coat, feeling sure I should not be able to get it on again. It was while we were eating our bread that the rumour first reached us of another disaster, even greater than that we had witnessed ourselves. Whence it came I know not; but a whisper went down the ranks that Woolwich had been captured. We all knew that it was our only arsenal, and understood the significance of the blow. No hope, if this were true, of saving the country. Thinking over this, we went back to the shed...

F

Although this was only our second day of war,
I think we were already old soldiers so far that we
had come to be careless about fire, and the shot
and shell that now began to open on us made no
sensation. We felt, indeed, our need of discipline,
and we saw plainly enough the slender chance of
success coming out of troops so imperfectly
trained as we were; but I think we were all determined to fight on as long as we could. Our
gallant adjutant gave his spirit to everybody;
and the staff-officer commanding was a very
cheery fellow, and went about as if we were
certain of victory. Just as the firing began he
looked in to say that we were as safe as in a church,
that we must be sure and pepper the enemy well,
and that more cartridges would soon arrive.
There were some steps and benches in the shed,
and on these a party of our men were standing, to
fire through the upper loop-holes, while the line
soldiers and others stood on the ground, guarding
the second row. I sat on the floor, for I could
not now use my rifle, and besides, there
were more men than loop-holes. The artillery
fire which had opened now on our position was
from a longish range; and occupation for the
riflemen had hardly begun when there was a crash
in the shed, and I was knocked down by a blow on
the head. I was almost stunned for a time, and
could not make out at first what had happened.
A shot or shell had hit the shed without quite
penetrating the wall, but the blow had upset the

steps resting against it, and the men standing on them, bringing down a cloud of plaster and brickbats; one of which had struck me. I felt now past being of use. I could not use my rifle, and could barely stand ; and after a time I thought I would make for my own house, on the chance of finding some one still there. I got up therefore, and staggered homewards. Musketry fire had now commenced, and our side were blazing away from the windows of the houses, and from behind walls, and from the shelter of some trucks still standing in the station. A couple of field-pieces in the yard were firing, and in the open space in rear of the station a reserve was drawn up. There, too, was the staff-officer on horseback, watching the fight through his field-glass. I remember having still enough sense to feel that the position was a hopeless one. That straggling line of houses and gardens would surely be broken through at some point, and then the line must give way like a rope of sand. It was about a mile to our house, and I was thinking how I could possibly drag myself so far when I suddenly recollected that I was passing Travers's house,—one of the first of a row of villas then leading from the Surbiton station to Kingston. Had he been brought home, I wondered, as his faithful old servant promised, and was his wife still here ? I remember to this day the sensation of shame I felt, when I recollected that I had not once given him—my greatest friend—a thought since I carried him off the field the day before.

But war and suffering make men selfish. I would
go in now at any rate and rest awhile, and see if
I could be of use. The little garden before the
house was as trim as ever—I used to pass it every
day on my way to the train, and knew every shrub
in it—and ablaze with flowers, but the hall-door
stood ajar. I stepped in and saw little Arthur
standing in the hall. He had been dressed as
neatly as ever that day, and as he stood there in
his pretty blue frock and white trousers and socks
showing his chubby little legs, with his golden
locks, fair face, and large dark eyes, the picture of
childish beauty, in the quiet hall, just as it used
to look—the vases of flowers, the hat and coats
hanging up, the familiar pictures on the walls—
this vision of peace in the midst of war made me
wonder for a moment, faint and giddy as I was,
if the pandemonium outside had any real existence, and was not merely a hideous dream. But
the roar of the guns making the house shake, and
the rushing of the shot, gave a ready answer. The
little fellow appeared almost unconscious of the
scene around him, and was walking up the stairs
holding by the railing, one step at a time, as I had
seen him do a hundred times before, but turned
round as I came in. My appearance frightened
him, and staggering as I did into the hall, my face
and clothes covered with blood and dirt, I must
have looked an awful object to the child, for he
gave a cry and turned to run toward the basement
stairs. But he stopped on hearing my voice calling

him back to his god-papa, and after a while came
timidly up to me. Papa had been to the battle,
he said, and was very ill : mamma was with papa :
Wood was out : Lucy was in the cellar, and had
taken him there, but he wanted to go to mamma.
Telling him to stay in the hall for a minute till I
called him, I climbed upstairs and opened the
bedroom door. My poor friend lay there, his body
resting on the bed, his head supported on his wife's
shoulder as she sat by the bedside. He breathed
heavily, but the pallor of his face, the closed eyes,
the prostrate arms, the clammy foam she was
wiping from his mouth, all spoke of approaching
death. The good old servant had done his duty,
at least,—he had brought his master home to die
in his wife's arms. The poor woman was too in-
tent on her charge to notice the opening of the door
and as the child would be better away, I closed it
gently and went down to the hall to take little
Arthur to the shelter below, where the maid was
hiding. Too late! He lay at the foot of the stairs
on his face, his little arms stretched out, his hair
dabbled in blood. I had not noticed the crash
among the other noises, but a splinter of a shell
must have come through the open doorway ; it
had carried away the back of his head. The poor
child's death must have been instantaneous. I
tried to lift up the little corpse with my one arm,
but even this load was too much for me, and while
stooping down I fainted away.

When I came to my senses again it was quite

dark, and for some time I could not make out where I was; I lay indeed for some time like one half asleep, feeling no inclination to move. By degrees I became aware that I was on the carpeted floor of a room. All noise of battle had ceased, but there was a sound as of many people close by. At last I sat up and gradually got to my feet. The movement gave me intense pain; for my wounds were now highly inflamed, and my clothes sticking to them made them dreadfully sore. At last I got up and groped my way to the door, and opening it at once saw where I was, for the pain had brought back my senses. I had been lying in Travers's little writing-room at the end of the passage, into which I made my way. There was no gas, and the drawing-room door was closed; but from the open dining-room the glimmer of a candle feebly lighted up the hall, in which half-a-dozen sleeping figures could be discerned, while the room itself was crowded with men. The table was covered with plates, glasses, and bottles; but most of the men were asleep in the chairs or on the floor, a few were smoking cigars, and one or two with their helmets on were still engaged at supper, occasionally grunting out an observation between the mouthfuls.

"Sind wackere Soldaten, diese Englischen Freiwilligen," said a broad-shouldered brute, stuffing a great hunch of beef into his mouth with a silver fork, an implement I should think he must have been using for the first time in his life.

" Ja, ja," replied a comrade, who was lolling
back in his chair with a pair of very dirty legs on
the table, and one of poor Travers's best cigars in
his mouth ; " Sie so gut laufen können."

" Ja wohl," responded the first speaker ; " aber
sind nicht eben so schnell wie die Französischen
Mobloten."

" Gewiss," grunted a hulking lout from the
floor, leaning on his elbow, and sending out a cloud
of smoke from his ugly jaws ; " und da sind hier
etwa gute Schützen."

" Hast recht, lange Peter," answered number
one ; "-wenn die Schurken so gut exerciren wie
schützen könnten, so wären wir heute nicht hier! "

" Recht! recht! " said the second ; " das
exerciren macht den guten Soldaten."

What more criticisms on the shortcomings of
our unfortunate volunteers might have passed I
did not stop to hear, being interrupted by a sound
on the stairs. Mrs. Travers was standing on the
landing-place ; I limped up the stairs to meet her.
Among the many pictures of those fatal days
engraven on my memory, I remember none more
clearly than the mournful aspect of my poor
friend, widowed and childless within a few
moments, as she stood there in her white dress,
coming forth like a ghost from the chamber of the
dead, the candle she held lighting up her face, and
contrasting its pallor with the dark hair that fell
disordered round it, its beauty radiant even
through features worn with fatigue and sorrow.

She was calm and even tearless, though the trembling lip told of the effort to restrain the emotion she felt. " Dear friend," she said, taking my hand, " I was coming to seek you ; forgive my selfishness in neglecting you so long ; but you will understand "—glancing at the door above—" how occupied I have been." " Where," I began, " is "——" my boy ? " she answered, anticipating my question. " I have laid him by his father. But now your wounds must be cared for ; how pale and faint you look!—rest here a moment,"—and, descending to the dining-room, she returned with some wine, which I gratefully drank, and then, making me sit down on the top step of the stairs, she brought water and linen, and, cutting off the sleeve of my coat, bathed and bandaged my wounds. 'Twas I who felt selfish for thus adding to her troubles ; but in truth I was too weak to have much will left, and stood in need of the help which she forced me to accept ; and the dressing of my wounds afforded indescribable relief. While thus tending me, she explained in broken sentences how matters stood. Every room but her own, and the little parlour into which with Wood's help she had carried me, was full of soldiers. Wood had been taken away to work at repairing the railroad, and Lucy had run off from fright ; but the cook had stopped at her post, and had served up supper and opened the cellar for the soldiers' use : she herself did not understand what they said, and they were rough and boorish, but not uncivil. I

should now go, she said, when my wounds were
dressed, to look after my own home, where I might
be wanted; for herself, she wished only to be
allowed to remain watching there—glancing at
the room where lay the bodies of her husband and
child—where she would not be molested. I felt
that her advice was good. I could be of no use as
protection, and I had an anxious longing to know
what had become of my sick mother and sister;
besides, some arrangement must be made for the
burial. I therefore limped away. There was no
need to express thanks on either side, and the
grief was too deep to be reached by any outward
show of sympathy,

Outside the house there was a good deal of
movement and bustle; many carts going along,
the waggoners, from Sussex and Surrey, evidently
impressed and guarded by soldiers; and although
no gas was burning, the road towards Kingston
was well lighted by torches held by persons
standing at short intervals in line, who had been
seized for the duty, some of them the tenants of
neighbouring villas. Almost the first of these
torch-bearers I came to was an old gentleman
whose face I was well acquainted with, from having frequently travelled up and down in the same
train with him. He was a senior clerk in a Government office, I believe, and was a mild-looking old
man with a prim face and a long neck, which he
used to wrap in a white double neckcloth, a thing
even in those days seldom seen. Even in that

moment of bitterness. I could not help being amused by the absurd figure this poor old fellow presented, with his solemn face and long cravat doing penance with a torch in front of his own gate, to light up the path of our conquerors. But a more serious object now presented itself, a corporal's guard passing by, with two English volunteers in charge, their hands tied behind their backs. They cast an imploring glance at me, and I stepped into the road to ask the corporal what was the matter, and even ventured, as he was passing on, to lay my hand on his sleeve. "Auf dem Wege, Spitzbube!" cried the brute, lifting his rifle as if to knock me down. "Must one prisoners who fire at us let shoot," he went on to add; and shot the poor fellows would have been, I suppose, if I had not interceded with an officer, who happened to be riding by. "Herr Hauptmann," I cried, as loud as I could, "is this your discipline, to let unarmed prisoners be shot without orders?" The officer, thus appealed to, reined in his horse, and halted the guard till he heard what I had to say. My knowledge of other languages here stood me in good stead, for the prisoners, north-country factory hands apparently, were of course utterly unable to make themselves understood, and did not even know in what they had offended. I therefore interpreted their explanation: they had been left behind while skirmishing near Ditton, in a barn, and coming out of their hiding-place in the midst of a party of the

enemy, with their rifles in their hands, the latter
thought they were going to fire at them from
behind. It was a wonder they were not shot down
on the spot. The captain heard the tale, and then
told the guard to let them go, and they slunk off
at once into a by-road. He was a fine soldier-like
man, but nothing could exceed the insolence of his
manner, which was perhaps all the greater because
it seemed not intentional, but to arise from a sense
of immeasurable superiority. Between the lame
freiwilliger pleading for his comrades, and the
captain of the conquering army, there was, in his
view, an infinite gulf. Had the two men been
dogs, their fate could not have been decided more
contemptuously. They were let go simply because
they were not worth keeping as prisoners, and
perhaps to kill any living thing without cause
went against the *hauptmann's* sense of justice.
But why speak of this insult in particular? Had
not every man who lived then his tale to tell of
humiliation and degradation? For it was the
same story everywhere. After the first stand in
line, and when once they had got us on the march,
the enemy laughed at us. Our handful of regular
troops was sacrificed almost to a man in a vain
conflict with numbers; our volunteers and
militia, with officers who did not know their work,
without ammunition or equipment, or staff to
superintend, starving in the midst of plenty, we
had soon become a helpless mob, fighting desper-
ately here and there, but with whom, as a man-

œuvring army, the disciplined invaders did just
what they pleased. Happy those whose bones
whitened the fields of Surrey; they at least were
spared the disgrace we lived to endure. Even you,
who have never known what it is to live otherwise
than on sufferance, even your cheeks burn when
we talk of these days; think, then, what those
endured who, like your grandfather, had been
citizens of the proudest nation on earth, which had
never known disgrace or defeat, and whose boast
it used to be that they bore a flag on which the sun
never set! We had heard of generosity in war; we
found none : the war was made by us, it was said,
and we must take the consequences. London and,
our only arsenal captured, we were at the mercy
of our captors, and right heavily did they tread
on our necks. Need I tell you the rest ?—of the
ransom we had to pay, and the taxes raised to
cover it, which keep us paupers to this day ?—the
brutal frankness that announced we must give
place to a new naval Power, and be made harmless
for revenge ?—the victorious troops living at free
quarters, the yoke they put on us made the more
galling that their requisitions had a semblance of
method and legality ? Better have been robbed at
first hand by the soldiery themselves, than through
our own magistrates made the instruments for
extortion. How we lived through the degradation
we daily and hourly underwent, I hardly even now
understand. And what was there left to us to live
for ? Stripped of our colonies ; Canada and the

West Indies gone to America ; Australia forced to
separate ; India lost for ever, after the English
there had all been destroyed, vainly trying to hold
the country when cut off from aid by their countrymen ; Gibraltar and Malta ceded to the new naval
Power ; Ireland independent and in perpetual
anarchy and revolution. When I look at my
country as it is now—its trade gone, its factories
silent, its harbours empty, a prey to pauperism
and decay—when I see all this, and think what
Great Britain was in my youth,—I ask myself
whether I have really a heart or any sense of
patriotism that I should have witnessed such
degradation and still care to live ! France was
different. There, too, they had to eat the bread
of tribulation under the yoke of the conqueror !
their fall was hardly more sudden or violent than
ours ; but war could not take away their rich soil ;
they had no colonies to lose ; their broad lands,
which made their wealth, remained to them ; and
they rose again from the blow. But our people
could not be got to see how artificial our prosperity
was—that it all rested on foreign trade and
financial credit ; that the course of trade once
turned away from us, even for a time, it might
never return ; and that our credit once shaken
might never be restored. To hear men talk in
those days, you would have thought that Providence had ordained that our Government should
always borrow at 3 per cent., and that trade
came to us because we lived in a foggy little island

set in a boisterous sea. They could not be got to
see that the wealth heaped up on every side was
not created in the country, but in India and China,
and other parts of the world ; and that it would
be quite possible for the people who made money
by buying and selling the natural treasures of the
earth, to go and live in other places, and take
their profits with them. Nor would men believe
that there could ever be an end to our coal and
iron, or that they would get to be so much dearer
than the coal and iron of America that it would no
longer be worth while to work them, and that
therefore we ought to insure against the loss of our
artificial position as the great centre of trade, by
making ourselves secure and strong and respected.
We thought we were living in a commercial
millennium, which must last for a thousand years
at least. After all, the bitterest part of our reflection is, that all this misery and decay might have
been so easily prevented, and that we brought it
about ourselves by our own shortsighted reckless-
ness. There, across the narrow Straits, was the
writing on the wall, but we would not choose to
read it. The warnings of the few were drowned in
the voice of the multitude. Power was then
passing away from the class which had been used
to rule, and to face political dangers, and which
had brought the nation with honour unsullied
through former struggles, into the hands of the
lower classes, uneducated, untrained to the use of
political rights, and swayed by demagogues ; and

the few who were wise in their generation were
denounced as alarmists, or as aristocrats who
sought their own aggrandisement by wasting
public money on bloated armaments. The rich
were idle and luxurious; the poor grudged the
cost of defence. Politics had become a mere
bidding for Radical votes, and those who should
have led the nation stooped, rather to pander to
the selfishness of the day, and humoured the
popular cry which denounced those who would
secure the defence of the nation by enforced
arming of its manhood, as interfering with the
liberties of the people. Truly the nation was ripe
for a fall; but when I reflect how a little firmness
and self-denial, or political courage and foresight,
might have averted the disaster, I feel that the
judgment must have really been deserved. A
nation too selfish to defend its liberty, could not
have been fit to retain it. To you, my grandchildren, who are now going to seek a new home
in a more prosperous land, let not this bitter
lesson be lost upon you in the country of your
adoption. For me, I am too old to begin life again
in a strange country; and hard and evil as have
been my days, it is not much to await in solitude
the time which cannot now be far off, when my old
bones will be laid to rest in the soil I have loved so
well; and whose happiness and honour I have so
long survived.

GARDEN CITY PRESS
LIMITED PRINTERS
LETCHWORTH, HERTS

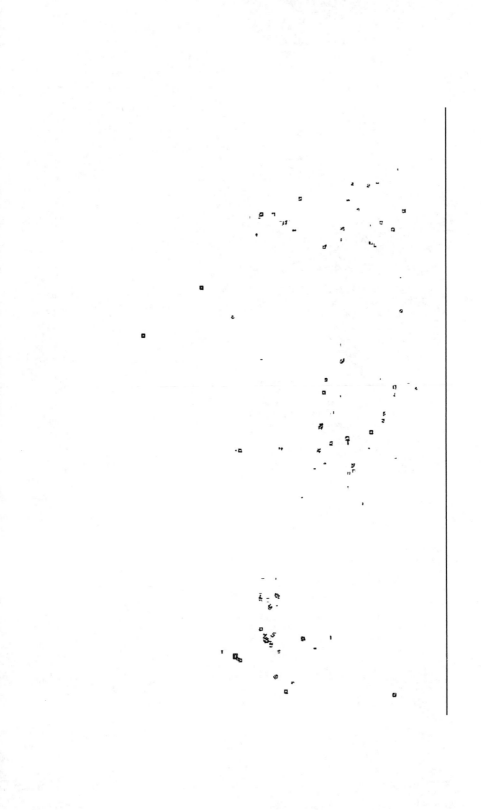

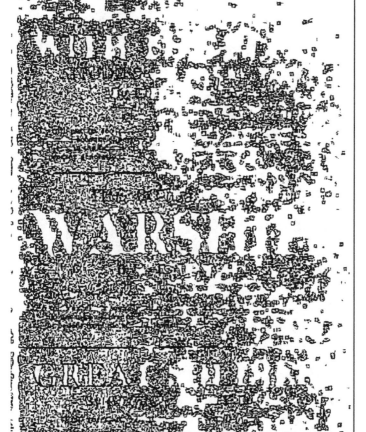

9 781375 869942